P9-DEI-678

The Great Alignment

The Great Alignment

Race, Party Transformation,
and the Rise of Donald Trump

Alan I. Abramowitz

Yale UNIVERSITY PRESS

New Haven & London

Published with assistance from the foundation established in memory of
Philip Hamilton McMillan of the Class of 1894, Yale College.

Copyright © 2018 by Alan I. Abramowitz.
All rights reserved.
This book may not be reproduced, in whole or in part, including illustrations,
in any form (beyond that copying permitted by Sections 107 and 108 of the
U.S. Copyright Law and except by reviewers for the public press), without
written permission from the publishers.

Yale University Press books may be purchased in quantity for educational,
business, or promotional use. For information, please e-mail
sales.press@yale.edu (U.S. office) or sales@yaleup.co.uk (U.K. office).

Set in Janson Roman type by Integrated Publishing Solutions,
Grand Rapids, Michigan.
Printed in the United States of America.

ISBN 978-0-300-20713-2 (hardcover : alk. paper)
Library of Congress Control Number: 2017961074
A catalogue record for this book is available from the British Library.

This paper meets the requirements of ANSI/NISO Z39.48-1992
(Permanence of Paper).

10 9 8 7 6 5 4 3 2 1

To Ann

Contents

Contents

Preface

On January 20, 2017, Donald Trump was inaugurated as the forty-fifth president of the United States. The next day, millions of Americans turned out to protest Trump's presidency in rallies and marches across the nation. Hundreds of thousands showed up to march in Washington, D.C., but there were protest marches in almost every major city in the United States and in dozens of smaller cities and towns, from Huntington, West Virginia, to Oklahoma City, Oklahoma, to Fairbanks, Alaska.

In the first Gallup Poll measuring Trump's approval rating as president, three days after his inauguration, 45 percent of Americans approved of his performance and 45 percent disapproved. Trump's initial approval rating was the lowest in the history of the Gallup Poll; his initial disapproval rating was by far the highest in the poll's history. Just as striking, though, was the sharp partisan divide in these ratings—90 percent of Republicans approved of Trump's performance, while 81 percent of Democrats disapproved. In the United States Senate, Democrats and Republicans quickly found themselves battling over President Trump's choices for key Cabinet positions, with several, including his nominees for attorney general and secretary of state, winning approval on party-line or near party-line votes.

In an era marked by deep partisan divisions, Donald Trump may well be the most divisive political leader in modern American history. Nevertheless, while Trump won the election by exploiting the deep divisions in American society, he did not create those divisions. The deep racial, cultural, and ideological schisms exposed by Trump's candidacy have been developing for decades, and regardless of the course of his presidency, whether he succeeds beyond the wildest expectations of his supporters or fails miserably, they are not going away any time soon.

The central argument of this book is that the deep partisan divide that exists among the politically engaged segment of the American public as well as among political elites and activists is, fundamentally, a disagreement over the dramatic changes that have transformed American society and culture since the end of World War II, and that continue to have huge effects in the twenty-first century. The challenges posed by technological change, globalization, immigration, growing racial and ethnic diversity, and changes in family structure and gender roles have produced diverging responses from party elites and a growing alignment of partisan identities with deeper divisions in American society and culture. This "great alignment" has transformed the American party system and fundamentally altered American politics in the twenty-first century.

On one side of this partisan divide are those who have benefited from and welcome the new American society, including racial minorities, the LGBT community, religious moderates and skeptics, and more educated citizens who possess the skills to thrive in the economy of the twenty-first century. Those Americans voted overwhelmingly for Barack Obama in 2008 and 2012 and for Hillary Clinton in 2016. On the other side of the divide are those who find these changes deeply troubling and threatening, including religious conservatives and many less educated whites in small towns and rural areas. Those Americans voted overwhelmingly for John McCain in 2008, Mitt Romney in 2012, and Donald Trump in 2016.

With the nation almost evenly divided between supporters of the two sides, relatively small shifts in party allegiance or turnout can produce different outcomes and dramatic swings in the direction of public policy. Short-term forces still matter in elections, as the response of the public to the economic crisis posed by the Great Recession demonstrated in 2008. However, the great alignment has produced a sharply polarized electorate marked by deep hostility among partisans on both sides toward the other party and its leaders. The rise of "negative partisanship" has resulted in growing party loyalty, straight-ticket voting, and the increasing nationalization of sub-presidential elections. It also contributed to the improbable rise and ultimate victory of Donald Trump—a candidate who overcame strong opposition from many Republican Party leaders and elected officials and serious reservations among many Republican voters by exploiting fear and hatred of Democrats in general and Hillary Clinton in particular.

The great alignment has had profound consequences for almost every aspect of American politics. For one thing, it has resulted in a growing nationalization of party politics and electoral competition. The late House Speaker Tip O'Neill's famous statement that "all politics is local" has been stood on its head. Today, it would be more accurate to say that all politics is national. Dramatic increases in party loyalty and straight-ticket voting mean that the outcomes of elections at every level from the U.S. Senate and House down to local offices are closely tied to the results of presidential elections. As a result, the personalities and records of individual candidates mean far less than they did in the past.

The main beneficiary of this trend has been the Republican Party.

Because of the heavy concentration of Democratic voting groups in large metropolitan areas, Republicans have long enjoyed an advantage in the number of congressional and state legislative districts that tilt toward the GOP in presidential elections—an advantage that had nothing to do with partisan gerrymandering. As recently as the 1990s, however, high rates of ticket splitting allowed Democrats to hold on to a large share of these districts. The increase in straight-ticket voting means that is no longer the case. In recent elections to the House of Representatives, over 90 percent of contests have been won by the candidate of the party carrying the district in the presidential election.

A similar trend is apparent in recent Senate elections. Each party now holds the large majority of seats in states won by its presidential candidate. But sparsely populated rural states are greatly overrepresented in the Senate, and most of those states now tilt toward the GOP. Moreover, this Republican advantage affects presidential elections, since each state's two U.S. senators count in determining its electoral votes. In a nation that is becoming increasingly urbanized, and in which urbanization is highly correlated with partisanship, this GOP advantage is a source of growing frustration for Democratic leaders and voters.

Perhaps the most important and potentially dangerous long-term consequence of the great alignment has been the increasing centrality of issues of race and ethnicity in American politics. No other development in American politics has had a greater impact on the rise of partisan polarization over the past thirty years. Supporters of the two major parties are increasingly divided by race and ethnicity. More important, they are increasingly divided by their attitudes toward race and ethnicity, and attitudes toward race and ethnicity are increasingly connected with attitudes toward other major issues in American politics, including the role of government and the state of the economy.

Preface

Donald Trump's strong showing among white working-class voters in 2016 has sparked a debate among journalists and scholars about the relative importance of economic grievances and racial attitudes in attracting support for Trump among these voters. The evidence presented in this book, however, demonstrates that economic and racial attitudes are closely connected, and that among Trump supporters, economic grievances are driven more by racial and ethnic resentment than by economic conditions. How these voters and their communities are faring seems to matter less in shaping their political outlook than whom they blame for their problems.

Acknowledgments

Many individuals have influenced my ideas on the transformation of the American party system, the rise of negative partisanship, and the nationalization of elections in the United States over the past several decades. I owe a considerable debt of gratitude to my collaborator, coauthor, and methods tutor on several recent projects, Steven Webster. I have also been greatly influenced by the writings of other scholars on partisan polarization and its consequences, including Larry Sabato, Kyle Saunders, Ron Rapoport, Walter Stone, Gary Jacobson, James Campbell, Norman Ornstein, Thomas Mann, and Bill Bishop. William Frucht, the political science editor at Yale University Press, has provided constant encouragement and much helpful feedback during the writing of this book. Finally, I want to thank my students at Emory University for the past thirty years. Their interest and curiosity about the political world have been a source of constant intellectual stimulation.

This book is dedicated to Ann Abramowitz, who provided not

only encouragement and support for this project but invaluable in-
struction on how national political forces were playing out in our
own state and community based on her deep involvement in the
political process.

The Great Alignment

ONE

A New Age of Partisanship

In the twenty-first century, the United States entered a new age of partisanship. Sharp party divisions now characterize all of the nation's major political institutions. In Congress, the ideological divide between Democrats and Republicans in both the House and the Senate is larger than at any time in the past century.[1] Party unity on roll-call votes has increased dramatically in both chambers since the 1970s.[2] On the Supreme Court, the justices now divide along party lines on major cases with greater frequency than at any time in decades.[3] In many of the states, Democrats and Republicans are even more deeply divided along ideological lines than they are in Congress.[4]

It has become obvious to both scholarly and non-scholarly observers that partisan conflict among political elites has greatly intensified. What is not as widely acknowledged is that polarization is not confined to the elites. The American people—especially those who actively participate in politics—have also become polarized. Partisan polarization among political elites cannot be understood unless we take into account the parallel rise in polarization in the public as a whole.

The central argument of this book is that this polarization is not an elite phenomenon. Its causes can be found in dramatic changes in American society and culture that have divided the public into opposing camps—those who welcome those changes and those who feel threatened by them. This growing division within the public expresses itself in many parallel rifts—racial and ethnic, religious, cultural, geographic—and it has produced an electorate that is increasingly mistrustful of anyone in the other camp. Democratic and Republican elites are hostile toward members of the other party primarily because Democratic and Republican voters are hostile toward members of the other party. This mutual hostility and mistrust reached new heights in the extraordinarily bitter and divisive election of 2016, and even greater heights with the ascension of Donald Trump to the presidency.

These extremes of partisan behavior appear on almost every measure political scientists can devise. Among all types of party supporters—strong identifiers, weak identifiers, and leaning independents—party loyalty and straight-ticket voting in 2012 reached their highest levels in at least sixty years. According to data from the American National Election Study (ANES) of 2012, 91 percent of a party's supporters voted for their party's presidential candidate. That tied the record first set in 2004 and matched in 2008. The 90 percent rate of party loyalty in the House elections of 2012 tied the record set in 1956, and the 89 percent rate of party loyalty in the Senate elections the same year broke the previous record of 88 percent, set in 1958. Unsurprisingly, these rates of party loyalty were accompanied by very high levels of straight-ticket voting. The 89 percent rate of straight-ticket voting in the presidential and House elections in 2012 broke the record of 87 percent set in 1952, and the 90 percent rate of straight-ticket voting in the presidential and

Senate elections in 2012 broke the record of 89 percent set in 1960. These extraordinarily high rates of party loyalty continue a trend that has been evident since partisanship reached a low point in the 1970s and '80s.[5]

A related measure is how consistently party supporters and independents who lean toward one or the other party vote for their party's candidates for president, Senate, and U.S. House of Representatives in the same election. According to data from the ANES cumulative file, the proportion voting this way has increased dramatically since the 1970s. Among all party supporters, the rate of consistent loyalty in 2012 was an all-time record, at 81 percent, breaking the record of 79 percent set in 1960. This represented a sharp increase from the loyalty rates of 55 to 63 percent among all party supporters between 1972 and 1988. Republicans had a 79 percent rate of consistent loyalty in 2012, which was somewhat lower than their loyalty rates in 1952, 1956, and 1960, but substantially higher than the rates of the 1970s and 1980s. Democrats had an 84 percent rate of consistent loyalty in 2012, which was the highest ever seen in an ANES survey, easily surpassing the 80 percent recorded in 2004. And party loyalty has increased sharply among all types of partisans—more, in fact, among weak identifiers and leaning independents than among strong identifiers. Between 1980 and 2012, consistent loyalty rose from 71 percent to 89 percent among strong party identifiers, from 47 percent to 74 percent among weak party identifiers, and from 46 percent to 74 percent among leaning independents.

These trends appear to have continued in 2016 despite extraordinarily high negative ratings for both presidential candidates and despite the fact that the Republican nominee had been bitterly opposed by many prominent Republican Party leaders and office holders during the primary campaign. According to data from the national exit poll, over 90 percent of Democratic identifiers voted for Hillary Clinton, and over 90 percent of Republican identifiers voted for Donald Trump. Well over 90 percent of Clinton voters supported a Democratic candidate for the U.S. House, and well over 90 percent of Trump voters supported a Republican House candidate.

Partisan Behavior Versus Partisan Identification

Despite their partisan behavior, Americans seem increasingly unwilling to acknowledge any attachment to a political party. In the 2012 ANES survey, only 63 percent of voters identified as either Democrats or Republicans—the lowest percentage of party identifiers in the survey's history. Between 1952 and 1964, about 80 percent of voters identified with one of the two major parties. Even during the 1970s and 1980s, when party loyalty in voting was at its nadir, the percentage of party identifiers never fell below 66 percent. Moreover, the ANES surveys are not alone in picking up this trend. The Gallup Poll, using a slightly different question, also reports a substantial increase in the proportion of Americans calling themselves independents.[6]

It appears that many American voters today are reluctant to claim any affiliation with a political party. This may reflect a kind of social desirability effect. Because partisanship has a negative connotation, the independent label appeals to many voters: being an independent means thinking for oneself rather than voting blindly for one political party. However, when pressed about their party preference, most of these "independents" make it clear that they usually lean toward one of the two major parties. In recent elections, only about 12 percent of Americans have fallen into the "pure independent" category, and these people are much less interested in politics and much less likely to vote than independent leaners. When we shift our focus from partisan identification to partisan behavior, we find that leaning independents as well as strong and weak party identifiers are voting more along party lines than at any time in the past half century.

The Rise of Negative Partisanship

This surge in partisan behavior reflects a fundamental change in political identity in the American electorate, one not adequately captured by conventional measures of party identification: the rise of negative partisanship. Over the past two decades, the proportion of party supporters (including leaning independents) who have strongly negative feelings toward the opposing party has risen sharply. A growing number of Americans have been voting against the opposing party rather than for their own.

The rise of negative partisanship has brought a sharp increase in party loyalty at all levels, a concurrent increase in straight-ticket voting, and a growing connection between the results of presidential elections and those farther down the ballot. More than at any time since World War II, electoral results below the presidential level reflect the results of presidential elections.[7]

Over the past several decades, as partisan identities have become increasingly aligned with other social and political divisions, supporters of each party have come to perceive the other party's supporters as very different from themselves in values and social characteristics as well as political beliefs. This perception has reinforced their strongly negative opinions of the other party's elected officials, candidates, and supporters.[8] Such negative perceptions are further aggravated by partisan news sources.[9]

Favorability ratings by party supporters toward their own party and the opposing party, as reported in the ANES surveys, can be plotted graphically on a "feeling thermometer" scale. The feeling thermometer ranges from zero degrees, the most negative rating, to 100 degrees, the most positive. A rating of 50 is considered neutral. Since they were first asked the question, party supporters' rat-

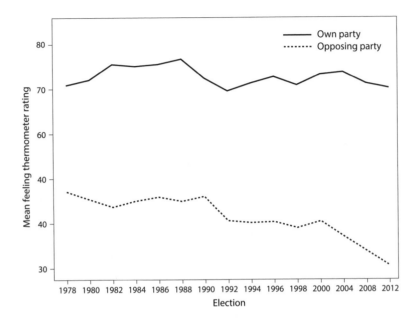

Figure 1.1. Ratings of Own Party and Opposing Party on Feeling Thermometer, 1978–2012. Source: ANES Cumulative File

ings of their own party have changed very little, moving from 71 degrees in 1978 to 70 degrees in 2012 (figure 1.1). But voters' ratings of the opposing party have fallen sharply, from 47 degrees in 1978 to 30 in 2012. Moreover, this increasing negativity affected all types of party supporters. Between 1978 and 2012 the mean rating of the opposing party on the feeling thermometer scale fell from 41 degrees to 24 among strong party identifiers, from 50 to 36 among weak party identifiers, and from 51 to 35 among leaning independents. In 1978, 63 percent of voters gave the opposing party a neutral or positive rating while only 19 percent gave the opposing party a rating of 30 degrees or lower. By 2012, only 26 percent of voters rated the opposing party as neutral or positive, while 56 percent gave it a rating of 30 degrees or lower.

Most of the shift toward negative partisanship has taken place since 2000. In the twelve years between 2000 and 2012 the proportion of positive partisans (voters who liked their own party more than they disliked the opposing party) fell from 61 percent to 38 percent, while the proportion of negative partisans (those who disliked the opposing party more than they liked their own) rose from 20 percent to 42 percent.[10] In 2012, for the first time since the ANES began asking the party feeling thermometer question, negative partisans outnumbered positive partisans.

Negative partisanship influences feelings about the presidential candidates as well. Over the past several decades, voters' ratings of their own party's presidential candidate have remained fairly steady, generally in the 70–75 degree range on the feeling thermometer. However, their ratings of the opposing party's candidate have declined sharply. In 1968, the first time the ANES asked for feeling thermometer ratings of presidential candidates, 51 percent of voters gave the opposing party's candidate a positive rating while only 19 percent gave him a rating of 30 degrees or lower. In 2012, only 15 percent of voters gave the opposing party's presidential candidate a positive rating; 60 percent rated him 30 degrees or lower.

These negative feelings only increased in 2016. According to a survey conducted by the Pew Research Center between September 27 and October 10, 2016, Democrats and Democratic-leaning independents gave Donald Trump a mean rating of just 10 degrees on the feeling thermometer. Fully 85 percent of Democrats gave Trump a rating below 50 degrees, with 77 percent rating him below 25 degrees on the 0–100 scale. Fifty-eight percent gave him a rating of zero. Likewise, Republican and Republican-leaning voters gave Clinton an average rating of 11 degrees. The vast majority of Republicans rated her below 25 degrees, including 56 percent who gave her a rating of zero.[11]

The rise of negative partisanship, and the growing divide between

Democrats and Republicans that it represents, have come alongside other, deeper divisions in American society: a racial divide between a shrinking white majority and a rapidly growing nonwhite minority, an ideological divide over the proper role and size of government, and a cultural divide over values, morality, and lifestyles. The past two decades have also seen the emergence of a large generational divide in American politics, because younger Americans are both more racially diverse and more liberal on social and cultural issues than older Americans. These deeper divides in American society have increased the disdain among each party's supporters for the supporters and leaders of the opposing party.

The Racial Divide

Perhaps the most important of these three divides is the one over race. Despite dramatic progress in recent decades, race and ethnicity still powerfully influence many aspects of American society, from housing patterns and educational opportunities to jobs and health care.[12] Moreover, since the 1980s, the racial divide has increasingly affected the American party system because of how racially conservative white voters have reacted to the growing racial and ethnic diversity of American society.[13]

Higher birth rates among nonwhites and high levels of immigration from Latin America and Asia have combined to create a steady increase in the nonwhite share of the U.S. population. This demographic shift has altered the racial composition of the American electorate as well, although at a slower rate due to nonwhites' lower levels of citizenship, voter registration, and turnout.[14] Nevertheless, between 1992 and 2008 the nonwhite share of the electorate doubled, from 13 percent to 26 percent. And contrary to the expectations of some conservative pundits and Republican strategists, the trend continued in 2012, with African-Americans, Hispanics, Asian-Americans, and other nonwhites making up a record 28 percent of the electorate, according to both the national exit poll and the 2012 ANES.[15] In 2016, according to the national exit poll, nonwhites made up 29 percent of the electorate.

As the nonwhite share of the electorate has grown, so has the racial divide between the Democratic and Republican coalitions. According to national exit poll data, between 1992 and 2016, the nonwhite share of Republican voters rose from 6 percent to 12 percent, while the nonwhite share of Democratic voters went from 21 percent to 45 percent. Data from the 2016 ANES show that this trend is almost certain to continue: the youngest members of the electorate are far more diverse than the oldest. According to the ANES data, nonwhites made up 39 percent of eligible voters under age thirty, compared with only 17 percent of eligible voters over seventy.

The racial divide between party coalitions has not been confined to presidential voters; it was just as large among voters in the U.S. House elections of 2016. In addition, the Democratic Party's growing dependence on nonwhite voters has contributed to the flight of racially and economically conservative white voters to the GOP, further widening the racial divide between the party coalitions. We will see that this growing racial divide set the stage for the rise of Donald Trump, who appealed to white racial resentment more openly than any major-party nominee in the postwar era.

The Ideological Divide

The Democrats' growing dependence on nonwhite voters and the flight of conservative whites to the Republicans have also contributed to the parties' growing ideological divide. Since at least the New Deal era, Democrats and Republicans have disagreed on the proper role and size of government. In recent years that ideological divide has widened, due mainly to the rightward drift of the GOP.[16]

The sharp partisan difference over the proper role of government was very evident in the 2012 and 2016 electorates. Data from the 2012 national exit poll show that 74 percent of Obama voters favored a more active role for the government in solving social problems, while 84 percent of Romney voters thought the government was already doing too many things that should be left to private individuals or businesses. Eighty-four percent of Obama voters wanted the Affordable Care Act preserved or expanded, while 89 percent of Romney voters wanted it partially or completely repealed. Finally, 83 percent of Obama voters favored increasing taxes on households with incomes over $250,000, compared with only 42 percent of Romney voters.[17] The results were very similar in 2016. According to national exit poll data, 75 percent of Clinton voters favored a more active role for the government in solving national problems and 87 percent wanted to see Obamacare maintained or expanded. In contrast, 78 percent of Trump voters favored a less active government role and 84 percent wanted Obamacare reduced in scope or eliminated.

The Cultural Divide

The cultural divide is the most recent source of difference between the parties, having begun to emerge only in the 1970s. Today, deeply felt moral and religious beliefs and lifestyle choices also make for a sharp contrast between Republicans and Democrats.[18] Building on a growing alliance with religious conservatives of all faiths and evangelical Protestants in particular, the Republican Party has become increasingly associated with policies that include restrictions on access to abortion and opposition to same-sex marriage and other legal rights for homosexuals. Meanwhile, the Democratic Party has gradually shifted to the left on these issues, perhaps most notably when President Obama himself finally announced his support for legalization of same-sex marriage in 2012.

Although the 2012 election was supposed to be all about jobs and the economy, cultural issues played a significant role. According to the national exit poll, white born-again or evangelical Christians made up 26 percent of the electorate, and despite any reservations they may have had about supporting a Mormon, they voted for Mitt Romney over Barack Obama by 78 percent to 21 percent. On the other hand, those who described their religious affiliation as "something else" or "none" made up 19 percent of the electorate, and they voted for Obama over Romney by an almost equally overwhelming margin, 72 percent to 25 percent. The 5 percent of voters who identified themselves as gay, lesbian, or bisexual supported Obama over Romney by 76 percent to 22 percent.

Just as on economic issues, Obama and Romney voters were sharply divided on cultural questions. Fully 84 percent of Obama voters wanted abortion to remain legal under all or most conditions, while 60 percent of Romney voters wanted to make it illegal under all or most conditions. More than three-quarters of Obama voters favored legalizing same-sex marriage in their own state, compared with only 26 percent of Romney voters.

Cultural issues contributed to two other striking voting patterns in 2012—the marriage gap and the generation gap. Unmarried voters and younger voters generally have more liberal cultural views than married and older voters. This helps explain the large gap in candidate preference between married and unmarried voters regardless of sex, and the large gap between voters under thirty and those sixty-five or older. According to the national exit poll, 60 percent of married men and 53 percent of married women voted for Romney, while 56 percent of unmarried men and 67 percent of unmarried women voted for Obama. Similarly, 60 percent of those under the age of thirty voted for Obama while 56 percent of those sixty-five or older voted for Romney.

The same patterns were clearly evident in 2016. According to data from the national exit poll, white born-again or evangelical voters favored Donald Trump over Hillary Clinton by 80 percent to 16 percent, while gay and lesbian voters favored Clinton over Trump by 77 percent to 14 percent. Similarly, according to data from the 2016 American National Election Study, voters who favored either an outright ban or very strict limits on access to abortion favored Trump over Clinton by 78 percent to 15 percent, while those who viewed abortion as a matter of personal choice for women favored Clinton over Trump by 61 percent to 31 percent.

The Great Alignment: Social Change and the Rise of Partisan Polarization

These divisions within the American electorate reflect dramatic changes in American society and culture since the 1960s. While political leaders have shaped voters' responses to these developments, they have not driven these responses or created the political landscape in which they themselves operate. The truth is the opposite: the country's radical social transformation has reshaped the Democratic and Republican electoral coalitions.

This transformation has included the civil rights revolution, the expansion of the regulatory and welfare state that was first created during the New Deal era, large-scale immigration from Latin America and Asia, the changing role of women, the changing structure of the American family, the women's rights and gay rights movements, and changing religious beliefs and practices. Compared with American society in the mid-twentieth century, the early twenty-first century version is much more racially and ethnically diverse, more dependent on government benefits, more sexually liberated, more religiously diverse, and more secular. It is also much more divided, and more bitterly divided, along party lines.

In general, Americans can be sorted into two camps: those who view the past half-century's changes as having mainly positive effects on their lives and on American society, and those who view the effects of these changes as mainly negative. Since the 1960s, Americans in the first group have increasingly come to support the Democrats, while those in the second group have increasingly come to support the Republicans. That, in a nutshell, is what has driven the realignment that has drastically remade the Democratic and Republican electoral coalitions.

The Democratic Party now draws its strongest support from the groups with the most positive views of recent social and cultural changes. These include nonwhites, immigrants, younger voters, single women, gays and lesbians, religious liberals, secular voters, those with a post-college education, and supporters of activist government. The Republican Party draws its strongest support from the groups with the most negative views of the same social and cultural changes. These groups are overwhelmingly white, and among whites, the Republican Party's strongest supporters today are older voters, evangelical Protestants and other religious conservatives, those without a college degree, and opponents of activist government.

Donald Trump's campaign slogan in 2016, "Make America Great Again," was aimed squarely at the latter group of voters. He promised to turn back the clock to a time when members of that group enjoyed greater influence and respect. In his campaign rhetoric and in his inaugural address, Trump constantly painted a portrait of a nation in steep decline—decline which only he could reverse. He repeatedly claimed, without evidence, that the unemployment rate in the United States was far higher than government statistics indicated, that violent crime in the nation's inner cities was soaring, and that the quality of most Americans' health care had deteriorated badly since the adoption of the Affordable Care Act. He portrayed Islamic terrorism as a dire threat to the lives of ordinary Americans, even though very few Americans had actually been killed or injured in Islamist terrorist attacks since 9/11.[19]

According to a survey conducted in August 2016 by the Pew

Research Center, a large majority of Trump's supporters shared his dark vision of the nation's condition and direction. Fully 81 percent of Trump supporters—compared with only 19 percent of Clinton supporters—believed that "life for people like them" had gotten worse in the past fifty years.[20] Moreover, the deep pessimism of Trump's supporters appears to have been based largely on unhappiness with the nation's changing demographics and values. Trump's appeals to racial resentment and xenophobia resonated with a large proportion of less-educated white voters who were uncomfortable with the increasing diversity of American society. Likewise, his promise to appoint conservative judges who would limit the rights of gays and lesbians and curtail access to abortion appealed to religious conservatives upset with the American public's growing liberalism on cultural issues. However, the message that was so welcome to large numbers of white working-class voters turned off overwhelming majorities of African-Americans, Latinos, Asian-Americans, and LGBT voters, along with many white college graduates, especially women, who benefited from and welcomed these changes.

In some cases, these social and cultural changes reinforced existing cleavages within the electorate; in other cases, they produced new cleavages. Democrats and Republicans have differed over the proper role and size of government since at least the 1930s, but this divide has deepened with the expansion of federal environmental, workplace, and consumer regulations and the creation of benefit programs such as food stamps, Medicare, Medicaid, and, most recently, Obamacare. The partisan differences over racial issues began to develop in the 1960s, when the old southern wing of the Democratic Party began defecting to the Republican side in response to the Democrats' support for the civil rights movement. Before then, both parties had been divided over racial equality—the Democrats perhaps more than the Republicans. Differences over cultural issues are even more recent, having first arisen in response to the Supreme

TABLE 1.1. DIVERGING ELECTORAL COALITIONS, 1972–2012

	Democratic voters		Republican voters	
	1972	2012	1972	2012
Nonwhites	17	42	3	12
White liberals	22	32	10	2
White moderates	43	21	42	18
White conservatives	18	6	45	68

Note: Entries shown are percentages. Respondents who opted out of ideology question are coded as moderates.

Sources: ANES Cumulative File

Court's decision in *Roe v. Wade*, which made abortion legal throughout the nation. The fight over abortion rights quickly became the template for other battles over changing societal norms and women's and gay people's demands for equality under the law—again, with Republicans and Democrats lining up on opposite sides with increasing uniformity.

What is striking in American politics today is the extent to which divisions on economic, racial, and cultural issues reinforce each other. Over the past several decades, racial, ideological, and cultural divisions in American society have created a growing divide between the electoral coalitions supporting the two major parties. Comparing the racial and ideological composition of the Democratic and Republican electoral coalitions in 1972 and 2012 shows very clearly that, in terms of race and ideology, the two coalitions have become much more distinct than they were forty years earlier (table 1.1). The contrast would undoubtedly be even greater if our data went back further, but unfortunately, the ANES survey used to gather this information from voters did not ask about respondents' ideology until 1972. We do, however, have data from ANES surveys on race and partisanship from the 1950s, and they show only a minimal racial divide between the party coalitions: whites made up 93 percent of Democratic voters and 97 percent of Republican voters.

Since the 1970s, both parties' electoral coalitions have changed dramatically. In 1972, white conservatives made up less than half of all Republican voters, and they barely outnumbered white moderates. Moderate plus liberal whites actually outnumbered conservative whites among Republican voters. By 2012, conservative whites made up more than two-thirds of Republican voters, greatly outnumbering moderate and liberal whites combined. The Republican Party's electoral base is thus much more conservative today than it was in 1972. In addition, while nonwhites form a slightly larger proportion of GOP voters today than they did in 1972, they remain a very small minority of Republican voters despite the dramatic increase in the minority share of the overall electorate.

African-Americans made up only one percent of Republican voters in 2012, compared with 23 percent of Democratic voters. Moreover, although nonwhite Republicans are somewhat more moderate than white Republicans, they are much more conservative than nonwhite Democrats. According to the 2012 ANES survey, 66 percent of nonwhite Republican voters described themselves as conservative, versus only 15 percent of nonwhite Democratic voters. Nonwhite Republicans were only slightly less conservative than white Republicans, and their presence in the party has very little impact on the overall conservatism of the modern GOP base.

The Democratic coalition has also undergone a makeover since 1972. In the case of the Democrats, the result has been to increase the influence of nonwhites and white liberals at the expense of moderate-to-conservative whites. In 1972, moderate-to-conservative whites made up about three-fifths of Democratic voters, but in 2012, they made up only about one-fourth of Democratic voters. Nonwhites and white liberals dominate today's Democratic coalition. While these two groups together made up only about two-fifths of Democratic voters in 1972, by 2012 they were about three-fourths of Democratic voters. Because of these changes, the center of gravity of the Democratic Party has shifted considerably to the left since the 1970s.

These changes in the Democratic and Republican coalitions have produced major shifts in how each party's supporters view those on the other side. To a much greater extent than thirty or forty years ago, Democrats and Republicans today see those who support the other party as very different from themselves, not only in their social characteristics and policy preferences but in their fundamental values. Ordinary Democrats and Republicans increasingly think the other party's supporters and leaders have questionable motives and pursue goals that would do grave harm to the country. According to a 2014 survey by the Pew Research Center, 27 percent of Democratic identifiers and leaners and 36 percent of Republican identifiers and leaners considered the opposing party "a threat to the nation." The hostility was even more intense among the most politically active party supporters—54 percent of Republican campaign contributors and 46 percent of Democratic campaign contributors thought of the opposing party as a threat to the nation.[21]

In every major political institution and at every level of government, the intensity of partisan conflict has increased dramatically, with major consequences for governance and public policy. In Washington, partisan polarization combined with divided party control has led to a politics of confrontation and gridlock. A growing number of state governments, meanwhile, are controlled by one party, with the result that Republican and Democratic states have moved in opposing directions on issues ranging from abortion and gun control to marriage equality and Medicaid expansion. It is no accident that some of the strongest resistance to the Trump administration's early decisions came from Democratic governors and attorneys general.

How We Got Here

Every party system builds on the one that preceded it. In order to understand the contemporary American party system, we must understand its predecessor and the forces that led to its collapse. In the next chapter, I will examine the demise of the New Deal party system forged by Franklin D. Roosevelt during the 1930s, which dominated American politics for more than thirty years. Roosevelt's electoral coalition was based on three major pillars: the white South, the heavily unionized northern white working class, and northern white ethnics. What united these groups politically was that they all benefited from FDR's New Deal policies.[22] After World War II, however, this coalition began to fracture under the impact of two dramatic changes in American society—the rise of a mass middle class, which turned many previous have-nots into people with a modicum of wealth, and the civil rights movement and consequent growth of the African-American electorate.

The Decline of the New Deal Coalition, 1952–1988

Between 1932 and 1936, Franklin Delano Roosevelt forged an electoral coalition that dominated American politics for more than half a century. In response to the Great Depression, and backed by huge Democratic majorities in the Senate and the House of Representatives, Roosevelt pushed through an ambitious legislative agenda that greatly enlarged the scope and power of the federal government. The New Deal did not end the economic crisis. That did not happen until the outbreak of World War II in Europe prompted the federal government to undertake a massive program of military mobilization and deficit spending, which it expanded after the U.S. entry into the war in late 1941. Yet even though it did not end the Great Depression, the New Deal alleviated the suffering of millions of Americans and gave them hope for a better future.[1]

At its core, Roosevelt's electoral coalition consisted of three groups that bore the brunt of the Great Depression—white southerners, northern white ethnics, and the northern white working class. His policies also appealed to another group that was very hard hit: African-Americans.[2] During the 1930s, for the first time since the Civil War, African-Americans began to switch their party allegiance from the Republican Party to the Democrats. For many years, however, the impact of this shift was limited because most African-Americans still resided in the states of the old Confederacy, where a combination of legal obstacles, economic pressures, and physical intimidation prevented most of them from voting.

The New Deal coalition gave Democrats the upper hand in American politics for more than fifty years. After Roosevelt's death, while the Democrats' dominance faded at the presidential level, it persisted for decades in Congress. Between 1949 and 1991, Democrats controlled the U.S. Senate for thirty-four of forty-two years and the House of Representatives for an astonishing forty of forty-two years. They also controlled most of the nation's governorships and state legislatures. Still, between 1949 and 1989, Republicans won seven of eleven presidential elections, and four of those seven victories—1952, 1956, 1972, and 1984—were double-digit landslides. Only one Democratic victory—Lyndon Johnson's defeat of Barry Goldwater in 1964—was a double-digit landslide.

The Democrats' weakness in presidential elections, a defining feature of the postwar era in American politics, led some observers to speculate that Republicans had developed a lock on the Electoral College.[3] Others saw an "emerging Republican majority," based on the movement of Americans from the cities to the suburbs and from the Frost Belt to the Sunbelt that would eventually make the GOP into the dominant party in congressional as well as presidential elections.[4]

Elections after 1988 showed that there was no emerging Republican majority and no GOP lock on the Electoral College. However, the difficulties Democratic presidential candidates had between the 1950s and the 1980s were an important indicator of the fragility of the New Deal coalition. The Democrats' major problem during this era, and especially after 1965, was finding a candidate who could hold together the disparate elements of the coalition. Once the immediate crisis of the Depression was over, conservative white southerners and ethnics began to realize that they had little in common with one another, or with the trade unionists and liberals who dominated the northern wing of the party.

To some extent, the Democrats were victims of their own success. The nation's rising affluence after World War II meant that many who had benefited from the New Deal began to see themselves less as beneficiaries of public spending than as taxpayers supporting programs that benefited others—others who increasingly looked different from themselves and whose lifestyles many found disturbing. For many members of the new white middle class, the issue behind much of the unease was race.

The movement of millions of African-Americans from the South to the major cities of the Northeast and Midwest between the 1930s and 1950s, and the rapid enfranchisement of millions of African-Americans in the South after the passage of the Voting Rights Act in 1965, fundamentally changed the Democratic electoral base. The presidential election of 1964 marked a major turning point in American politics when, for the first time, a Democratic president, Lyndon Johnson, promised to use the power of the federal government to advance the cause of civil rights for African-Americans. His Republican challenger, Barry Goldwater, strongly opposed any effort by the federal government to alter the racial status quo in the South.

Johnson benefited from a booming economy and widespread public sympathy following the assassination of President John F. Kennedy, winning a landslide victory and carrying forty-four of the fifty states. But of the six states that voted for Goldwater, five— Alabama, Mississippi, Georgia, South Carolina, and Louisiana— were in the South. (The sixth was his home state of Arizona.) It was the first time since the end of Reconstruction that a Republican presidential candidate carried the old Confederacy.[5] After 1964, African-American voters became the most reliably Democratic voting bloc in the nation and an increasingly important component of the party's electoral coalition. Meanwhile, southern whites, though they did not immediately abandon the Democrats below the presidential level, showed a growing inclination to vote Republican in presidential elections, especially when the Democratic candidate came from the party's liberal, northern wing. While it would take several decades for the South to become a Republican stronghold at all levels, the 1964 election clearly marked the end of the one-party Democratic South.[6]

The Parties in the Electorate, 1952–1960

In spite of Dwight D. Eisenhower's landslide victories over Adlai Stevenson in the presidential elections of 1952 and 1956, the data from the ANES surveys of 1952–1960 show that throughout this era, Democrats enjoyed a large and stable advantage over Republicans in party identification (table 2.1). In all three surveys, between 43 and 46 percent of voters identified with the Democratic Party, while 31 to 33 percent identified with the Republican Party. About 40 percent of voters identified strongly with a party, slightly fewer identified weakly with a party, and fewer than 25 percent of voters considered themselves independents. About the only things that changed between 1952 and 1960 were a small decline in the percentage of independents leaning toward the Democratic Party and a small increase in pure independents—voters with no party preference. These swings were much too small to change the overall picture of the electorate. Most voters readily identified with one of the two major parties, and the persistent effect of the New Deal realignment meant that many more identified as Democrats than as Republicans.

TABLE 2.1. PARTY IDENTIFICATION OF VOTERS
IN 1952, 1956, AND 1960 ELECTIONS

	1952	1956	1960
Strong Democrats	23	22	21
Weak Democrats	23	21	24
Leaning Democrats	10	6	6
Pure Independents	5	9	9
Leaning Republicans	8	9	8
Weak Republicans	14	15	15
Strong Republicans	17	17	18

Note: Entries shown are percentages. Totals may not equal 100 due to rounding error. Respondents classified as apolitical excluded.

Source: ANES Cumulative File

The lasting effects of the New Deal realignment can also be clearly seen in the size and party identification of several major demographic groups in the 1952–1960 ANES surveys (table 2.2). The most dramatic difference between the electorate of the 1950s and today's is its racial composition: the electorate of the 1950s was overwhelmingly white. The only significant nonwhite group was African-Americans—the ANES survey did not even count other racial groups until 1972. But while African-Americans made up about 9 percent of the voting-age population in these three elections, they were only 5 percent of the actual voters. Moreover, there was little difference between the Democratic and Republican coalitions. Both were overwhelmingly white: African-Americans made up only 6 percent of Democratic voters and just 2 percent of Republican voters.

During these years, despite the migration of millions of African-Americans from the South to the industrial states of the North, the greatest concentration of black citizens still lived in the southern states. According to the 1952–1960 ANES surveys, African-Americans made up almost one-fifth of the voting-age population

TABLE 2.2. PARTY IDENTIFICATION OF VOTING GROUPS, 1952–1960

Group (% of voters)	Democrats	Pure Independents	Republicans
All voters (100)	52	8	40
Blacks (5)	67	12	21
Whites (95)	52	7	41
Southern whites (17)	75	6	19
Northern whites (78)	47	8	46
Protestant (51)	35	7	58
Catholic (22)	68	8	24
Jewish (3)	76	8	16
Blue collar (23)	58	9	34
White collar (23)	40	7	53
Lower income (20)	48	7	45
Middle income (21)	50	8	42
Upper income (33)	45	8	48
No college (62)	51	8	41
College (16)	31	6	63
Union household (24)	61	7	31
Non-union (54)	40	8	52

Source: ANES Cumulative File

in the South during the 1950s compared with only 6 percent in the North. Even so, they constituted only 5 percent of actual voters in the eleven states of the old Confederacy. Before the Voting Rights Act of 1965, only 16 percent of southern blacks were able to overcome the numerous obstacles to registration and voting, and actually cast ballots.

That figure of 16 percent, however, conceals a dramatic difference in black voter participation between the Rim South and the Deep South.[7] In the Rim South states of Arkansas, Florida, North Carolina, Tennessee, Texas, and Virginia, where blacks made up only

13 percent of the voting-age population, 31 percent of African-Americans reported voting in presidential elections. Blacks made up about 6 percent of the electorate in these states. Things were very different in the Deep South states of Alabama, Mississippi, Georgia, South Carolina, and Louisiana. In these five states, where blacks made up a third of the voting-age population and were therefore a much greater potential threat to white political domination, they were almost completely disenfranchised. A combination of poll taxes, literacy tests, economic pressure, and physical intimidation kept almost all black citizens out of the voting booth. In these five states, only 4 percent of African-Americans reported voting in presidential elections in the 1950s, and blacks made up just 3 percent of voters. The region of the United States with by far the greatest concentration of African-American citizens had a nearly lily-white electorate.[8]

White southerners were the most Democratic voting group in the American electorate during this era: only 19 percent of southern whites identified with or leaned toward the Republican Party, while 75 percent identified with or leaned toward the Democrats. White southerners formed one of the largest components of the Democratic electoral coalition during the 1950s, making up almost one-fourth of all Democratic voters and outnumbering African-American voters by a four-to-one margin. It is easy to see why Democratic presidents and congressional leaders, fearful of alienating a core constituency, were reluctant to embrace the cause of civil rights.

The other major pillars of Roosevelt's New Deal coalition were northern white ethnics and northern white working-class voters, and both of these groups continued to identify with the Democratic Party by a wide margin during the 1950s. Democrats outnumbered Republicans among northern white Catholics and Jews by 44 points and 60 points, respectively. White blue-collar workers in the North backed Democrats by a 24-point margin, and members of white union households in the North backed them by a 30-point margin. On the other side, the most Republican voting groups in the nation were college-educated northern whites, a rather small group during that era, and the much larger group of northern white Protestants. Among northern white Protestants, Republicans outnumbered Democrats by 58 percent to 35 percent. Even so, northern white Protestants who were members of union households leaned Democratic by a margin of 49 percent to 43 percent. Among northern white Protestants who were not members of union households, Republicans outnumbered Democrats by 63 percent to 30 percent. White-collar workers in the North also favored Republicans during the 1950s, but by a narrower margin, 53 percent to 40.

During this era, northern white voters showed very little difference in party support based on family income. Republicans outnumbered Democrats by a margin of 51 percent to 43 percent among northern white voters with family incomes in the bottom sixth of the national income distribution. The only more Republican category was the very small group of voters in the top five percent of the income distribution, where Republicans outnumbered Democrats by 68 percent to 25 percent. The Democratic advantage among lower-middle- to upper-middle-income northern whites during this period may reflect the fact that many working-class voters, especially those who were unionized, enjoyed strong income gains during the postwar years. Only 15 percent of northern white voters in union households had family incomes in the bottom third of the national income distribution during the 1950s, compared with 32 percent of northern white voters who were not in union households.

The characteristics that did not divide Democrats and Republicans during the 1950s are just as revealing as those that did divide them. Democrats and Republicans in the 1950s were not divided by gender, marital status, or religiosity. The gender gap of the late twentieth and early twenty-first centuries, in which women were markedly more Democratic than men, did not exist in the '50s. In fact, women were slightly more Republican. Among men, Democrats outnumbered Republicans by 54 percent to 37 percent; among women, 51 percent to 42 percent.

There was also no marriage gap. The percentage of voters who were unmarried was much smaller than today—only 19 percent compared with 43 percent in the 2004–2012 elections. Moreover, instead of tilting Democratic, unmarried voters were somewhat more likely to identify as Republicans than married voters. Among married voters, Democrats outnumbered Republicans by 53 percent to 39 percent; among unmarried voters, 51 percent to 42 percent.

Finally, the "God gap" was also practically nonexistent. Very religious voters, unlike those today, did not tilt more toward the Republican Party than those who were less religious. Among voters who reported attending religious services regularly, Democrats outnumbered Republicans by 54 percent to 39 percent; among those who reported seldom or never attending religious services, the figures were 54 percent and 38 percent. The absence of a religiosity divide reflects the fact that issues such as abortion and gay rights had not yet emerged on the political scene.[9]

The most important difference between the American party system during the 1950s and that of today is that the parties in the fifties were much less ideologically aligned: liberals and conservatives were found in considerable numbers in both parties. Because of southern whites' traditional attachment to the Democratic Party and the exclusion of most African-Americans from the electorate, the Democratic coalition must have included a large proportion of conservative voters. Unfortunately, the ANES surveys did not yet ask voters their ideological leanings, mainly because the researchers who conducted these surveys assumed that few voters had them. In 1972, when the ANES did begin asking voters whether they called themselves conservative or liberal, the ideological divide between Democrats and Republicans turned out to be rather modest. It seems likely that it would have been even smaller in the 1950s.

Based on the distribution of party identification, the New Deal coalition seemed to be alive and well during the 1950s. All of the major voting groups that had supported Roosevelt during the 1930s and '40s continued to identify strongly with the Democratic Party, giving the Democrats a substantial advantage in party identification over Republicans. However, when it came to the actual election results, the picture was quite different. The regional and ideological diversity of the Democratic coalition made it hard for Democratic presidential candidates to hold them all together.

In both 1952 and 1956, massive Democratic defections enabled the Republican Eisenhower to defeat the Democrat Stevenson by landslide margins. In these two elections, according to the ANES data, between 25 and 30 percent of Democrats voted for Eisenhower, while fewer than 5 percent of Republicans voted for Stevenson. Even in 1960, when John F. Kennedy narrowly defeated Richard Nixon to take back the White House for the Democrats, 18 percent of Democrats defected to Nixon while only 8 percent of Republicans went to Kennedy.

In these three elections, Democrats suffered large-scale defections in almost every major voter group that made up Roosevelt's New Deal coalition. The only exception was Roman Catholics in 1960, who voted overwhelmingly for Kennedy, the first Catholic presidential candidate since 1928. The largest crack in the New Deal coalition during this era was found in the white South. In all three elections, southern whites defected at a noticeably higher rate than northern whites: the average defection rate in the two Eisenhower-Stevenson elections was 36 percent for southern whites versus 27 percent for northern whites. The difference was even greater in the 1960 Kennedy-Nixon contest: 32 percent for southern whites

TABLE 2.3. VOTING PATTERNS FOR PRESIDENT AND U.S. HOUSE, 1952–1960

Vote for Pres-House	All voters	Democrats	Republicans
D-D	41	73	4
D-R	3	4	1
R-D	11	13	7
R-R	45	10	88

Source: ANES Cumulative File

versus 14 percent for northern whites. The higher defection rate of southern whites suggests that there was an ideological component to Democratic defections, and even though ideological differences between the parties were muted, conservative Democrats were more likely to defect to Republican presidential candidates than liberal Democrats.

Despite the massive defections they suffered in these presidential elections, Democrats were able to win majorities in the U.S. Senate and House of Representatives in four of the five elections between 1952 and 1960, including the Eisenhower landslide of 1956. Looking at voting patterns for president and the House by party identification in the three presidential elections between 1952 and 1960 shows a trend toward asymmetric ticket splitting that would become even more pronounced in later elections (table 2.3). Only 14 percent of voters cast split-ticket ballots in the presidential and House contests during these years, but while 11 percent of voters chose a Republican presidential candidate and a Democratic House candidate, only 3 percent did the opposite. As a result, Democratic House candidates won an average of 52 percent of the vote in these elections, while Democratic presidential candidates won just 44 percent.

During the 1950s, Republicans displayed strong loyalty in both presidential and House elections, but they were somewhat more loyal in presidential elections—on average, 95 percent voted for Republican presidential candidates while 89 percent voted for Republican House candidates. Democrats, meanwhile, showed much greater loyalty in House elections than in presidential elections—an average of 86 percent voted for Democratic House candidates while only 77 percent voted for Democratic presidential candidates.

In congressional elections, Democrats could nominate candidates whose ideologies reflected the preferences of voters in each region. Democratic candidates in the South thus tended to be much more conservative than their counterparts in the North. This enabled Democrats to hold on to a majority of southern House and Senate seats until 1994. In presidential elections, however, Democrats could seldom find a single candidate who could appeal to their entire coalition. These difficulties became even greater after the passage of the Voting Rights Act in 1965, as the African-American electorate grew and Democratic candidates began openly courting the black vote.

1964: The Last Hurrah of the New Deal Coalition

In 1964, Lyndon Johnson put almost all of the pieces of FDR's coalition back together and won a landslide victory over Arizona senator Barry Goldwater. Aided by a booming economy and an opponent who frightened both Republicans and Democrats with his bellicose statements on foreign policy and his attacks on New Deal programs, Johnson carried forty-four states and led Democrats to major gains in the congressional elections. Republicans were reduced to their smallest numbers in the House and Senate since Roosevelt's 1936 landslide.[10]

For the first time in any ANES survey, Democrats in 1964 were more loyal to their party's presidential candidate than Republicans: 88 percent of Democrats voted for Johnson while only 75 percent of Republicans voted for Goldwater. Johnson's support was even greater among Democrats belonging to many of the core New Deal coalition groups: 93 percent of northern white Catholics, 95 percent of northern blue-collar workers, and 94 percent of northern whites in union households voted for him.

Only one major group from the New Deal coalition did not overwhelmingly support Johnson in 1964: white southerners. He won a majority of the vote among white southerners and carried six of the eleven states of the old Confederacy. However, according to the ANES survey, white southern Republicans were much more loyal to their party's nominee than white southern Democrats: 76 percent of the latter voted for Johnson while 93 percent of the former voted for Goldwater, whose inroads among white Democrats in the South were one of the few bright spots for Republicans in an otherwise disastrous election.

The Era of Dealignment: 1968–1988

The size and breadth of Johnson's victory led some political observers to speculate about a new era of Democratic domination, and perhaps even the demise of the GOP as a nationally competitive party. Such speculation proved to be premature. Only two years later, in the 1966 midterm election, Republicans gained forty-seven seats in the House and three seats in the Senate. Four years later, they took back the White House as the New Deal coalition splintered badly. In 1968, according to ANES data, 20 percent of Democrats voted for the Republican Richard Nixon and 12 percent voted for former Alabama governor George Wallace, a staunch opponent of federal civil rights laws who ran as an independent. Among white northern Democrats, 23 percent voted for Nixon and 7 percent for Wallace; among white southern Democrats, 20 percent voted for Nixon and an astonishing 40 percent for Wallace.[11] The Democrats did maintain control of both chambers of Congress, losing only five seats in the House and five seats in the Senate.

TABLE 2.4. VOTING PATTERNS FOR PRESIDENT AND U.S. HOUSE, 1968–1988

Vote for Pres-House	All voters	Democrats	Republicans
D-D	37	66	4
D-R	7	10	3
R-D	19	15	20
R-R	38	9	72

Source: ANES Cumulative File

From 1968 to 1988, Jimmy Carter was the only Democrat to win a presidential election—which he did once, in 1976. Of the other five presidential elections, four were Republican landslides. Yet Democrats controlled the House of Representatives throughout this period and the Senate for fourteen out of twenty years. As these results suggest, these two decades were the heyday of ticket splitting, as seen in the patterns of presidential and House voting during this era. On average, 26 percent of voters split their ticket for president and the House, almost double the 14 percent rate that prevailed between 1952 and 1960 (table 2.4). Moreover, the degree of asymmetry in ticket splitting was even more striking than during the fifties. Almost three times as many voters chose a Republican presidential candidate and a Democratic House candidate as did the reverse.

When we compare the voting patterns of Democrats and Republicans during this era, we see that Republicans were much more loyal than Democrats in presidential elections while Democrats were somewhat more loyal than Republicans in House elections. In presidential elections, Democrats defected at three times the rate of Republicans. On average, 92 percent of Republicans voted for Republican presidential candidates while only 76 percent of Democrats voted for Democratic presidential candidates. But in House elections, Republicans defected more frequently: 81 percent of Dem-

TABLE 2.5. PERCENTAGE OF VOTERS LOYAL TO PARTY
IN PRESIDENTIAL ELECTIONS, 1968–1988

Group	Democrats	Republicans
All voters	75	91
African-Americans	94	53
Whites	70	92
South	58	96
North	74	91
College	73	93
No college	69	91
Blue collar	70	89
White collar	72	93
Union household	75	90
Non-union household	68	92
Protestant	70	91
Catholic	74	90
Jewish	87	75
Liberal	87	80
Moderate, none	66	89
Conservative	53	96

Note: Based on votes for the two major parties. Data on ideology are for 1972–1988 elections only.

Source: ANES Cumulative File

ocrats voted for Democratic candidates but only 75 percent of Republicans voted for Republican candidates.

We can also compare the loyalty rates of various groups of Democratic and Republican voters in presidential elections between 1968 and 1988 (table 2.5). There were only three groups in which Democrats were more loyal than Republicans: African-Americans, Jews, and white self-identified liberals. These groups made up only a tiny fraction of the Republican electoral coalition because all three overwhelmingly identified with the Democratic Party. In sharp contrast, Republican loyalty greatly exceeded Democratic loyalty among voters in several groups that were major parts of the New Deal coalition, including white blue-collar voters, white members of union households, white Catholics and, most dramatically, white southerners. Between 1968 and 1988, only 58 percent of white southern Democrats, on average, voted for their party's presidential candidates, while 96 percent of white southern Republicans voted for their party's presidential candidates.

Democratic presidential candidates' difficulty in holding together the New Deal coalition was largely due to the coalition's ideological diversity. This can be seen very clearly in the rates of party loyalty among voters. Almost half of conservative Democrats and over a third of moderate Democrats in these elections voted for Republican presidential candidates. In contrast, the defection rate among liberal Democrats was only 13 percent. And while liberal Republicans also defected at a higher rate than moderate or conservative Republicans, they were a much smaller part of the Republican coalition—only 7 percent of Republican voters identified as liberals, while 18 percent of Democratic voters identified as conservatives—and liberal Republicans' defection rate was much lower than that of conservative Democrats.

Ideology largely explains the extraordinarily high defection rate among white southern Democrats in presidential elections. During this era, conservatives outnumbered liberals by 26 percent to 17 percent among white southern Democrats, while liberals outnumbered conservatives by 33 percent to 17 percent among white northern Democrats. Among the southerners, the defection rate in presidential elections between 1968 and 1988 averaged 58 percent among conservatives, 44 percent for moderates, and only 16 percent for liberals.

One of the most striking features of elections in the United States between 1968 and 1988 was the disconnect between presidential and congressional elections. Despite their difficulties in gaining the presidency, Democrats continued to enjoy considerable success in congressional elections. In eleven elections between 1968 and 1988, Democrats won an average of 60 percent of all House seats and 70 percent of southern House seats. They won an average of 57 percent of the vote in House elections during this era. However, that average conceals a wide variation: they won 70 percent of the vote in House elections in the South, but only 53 percent in House elections in the North. Thirty-eight percent of southern Republicans voted for Democratic House candidates, while only 14 percent of southern Democrats voted for Republican House candidates. In the North, Democratic and Republican defection rates were almost identical: 22 percent of Republicans voted for Democratic House candidates, and 20 percent of Democrats voted for Republican House candidates.

The explanation for southern Republicans' extraordinarily high defection rates during this era is very simple: incumbency. Comparing the defection rates of Democrats and Republicans in House elections between 1972 and 1988 by region and incumbency status shows that the higher loyalty rate of Democratic voters in the South was due entirely to the advantage of incumbency (table 2.6).[12] Democratic and Republican voters in both the South and the North were equally loyal in contests involving incumbents from their own party, open-seat contests, and contests involving the opposing party's incumbents. However, the proportion of Republican voters in districts with Democratic incumbents was much greater than the proportion of Democratic voters in districts with Republican incumbents, and this disparity was especially large in the South. Fifty-nine percent of southern voters lived in districts with Democratic incumbents, compared with only 51 percent of voters in the North; only 29 percent of voters in the South were in dis-

TABLE 2.6. PERCENTAGE OF VOTERS LOYAL TO PARTY IN U.S. HOUSE ELECTIONS
BY REGION AND INCUMBENCY STATUS OF CANDIDATES, 1972–1990

Group	Democrats	Republicans
All voters	82	73
Own party incumbent	94	94
Open seat	81	83
Opposing party incumbent	52	51
North		
Own party incumbent	93	94
Open seat	79	81
Opposing party incumbent	57	60
South		
Own party incumbent	94	90
Open seat	85	93
Opposing party incumbent	46	50

Note: Incumbency status of House candidates not available in ANES data before 1972

Source: ANES Cumulative File

tricts with Republican incumbents compared with 37 percent in the North.

Democratic control of the House of Representatives during this era was based on the ability of Democratic incumbents, especially southern Democratic incumbents, to win the support of Republican presidential voters. Between 1972 and 1988, an average of 30 percent of Republican presidential voters cast their ballots for Democratic House candidates; in districts with Democratic incumbents, 47 percent did so. In the North, an average of 28 percent of all Republican presidential voters and 43 percent of Republican presidential voters in districts with Democratic incumbents cast their ballots for Democratic House candidates. In the South, an average of 38 percent of all Republican presidential voters and 61 percent of Republican presidential voters in districts with Democratic incumbents cast their ballots for Democratic House candidates.

A key feature of the era of dealignment was voters' willingness to cross party lines to support incumbents from the opposing party in congressional elections. About half of voters in both parties defected to opposing-party incumbents in House elections during this era. However, the main beneficiaries of these defections were Democratic incumbents, who greatly outnumbered Republicans.

Many of these Democrats, especially in the South, were able to hold on to their seats even though the voters in their districts regularly supported Republican presidential candidates. In 1988, an astonishing 99 percent of incumbent Democrats in House districts carried by the Republican presidential candidate George H. W. Bush won reelection, including 54 of 55 incumbent Democrats in southern House districts carried by Bush. In the 101st Congress (1989–1991), 135 of 260 House Democrats, including 60 of 77 from the South, represented districts carried by the Republican presidential candidate in 1988.

As the 1980s ended, there was little reason to believe that the Democrats' domination of Congress was in danger. They had controlled the House for forty-five consecutive years and the Senate for thirty-nine of those forty-five years. In the 101st Congress, which was elected in 1988, they held 260 of 435 seats in the House and 55 of 100 seats in the Senate. Within a few years, however, two developments would bring the era of Democratic domination to an end—secular realignment within the electorate, and the nationalization of congressional elections.

Secular Realignment and the Transformation of the Party Coalitions

Democrats continued to outnumber Republicans in the American electorate during the 1980s. By the end of the decade, however, the Democratic advantage had decreased considerably. With leaning independents included with regular party identifiers, Democrats outnumbered Republicans by only three percentage points in 1984 and by two points in 1988. These were the first two surveys in the history of the ANES in which the Democratic advantage fell into the single digits.

Large as it was, the decline in the Democratic advantage in party identification between 1952 and 1988 does not show the true significance of changes in partisanship over these decades. For that, it is necessary to look at changes below the level of the entire electorate. There were dramatic differences in the direction and magnitude of change in party identification among major groups within the electorate, including some key parts of the New Deal coalition. The Democratic and Republican electoral coalitions of the late 1980s looked very different from the Democratic and Republican electoral coalitions of the 1950s (table 2.7).

By far the most important shift in the composition of the party coalitions involved race. Among white voters over these three decades, an 11-point Democratic advantage became a 10-point Republican advantage. Among African-American voters, a 46-point Democratic advantage became an 80-point Democratic advantage. At the same time, the nonwhite share of the electorate was growing steadily: African-Americans and other nonwhites went from only 5 percent of the electorate in the 1952–1960 elections to 18 percent in the 1984–1988 elections.

The result of these combined trends was a sharp increase in the racial divide between the parties. According to the ANES data, in the 1952–1960 elections, both parties' supporters were overwhelmingly white: nonwhites made up only 7 percent of Democratic voters and only 2 percent of Republican voters. By the 1984–1988 elections, nonwhites made up 29 percent of Democratic voters and 7 percent of Republican voters. During these years, nonwhite voters went from being a minor part of the Democratic electoral coalition to a large and important one.

TABLE 2.7. CHANGE IN PARTY IDENTIFICATION OF VOTER GROUPS
BETWEEN 1950S AND 1980S

Group	% Dem–% Rep		Change
	1952–1960	1984–1988	
All voters	+ 13	+ 3	– 10
Blacks	+ 46	+ 80	+ 34
Whites	+ 11	– 10	– 21
Southern whites	+ 55	– 2	– 57
Northern whites	+ 1	– 12	– 13
Protestant	– 23	– 32	– 9
Catholic	+ 44	+ 8	– 36
No college	+ 10	– 5	– 15
College	– 32	– 18	+ 14
White collar	– 13	– 16	– 3
Blue collar	+ 24	+ 2	– 22
Union household	+ 30	+ 15	– 15
Non-union household	– 12	– 21	– 9

Source: ANES Cumulative File

Between the 1952–1960 elections and those of 1984–1988, the Democratic advantage in party identification declined in every major white group of the traditional New Deal coalition, including northern white Catholics and blue-collar workers. By far the most dramatic change, however, involved the loyalties of southern whites. At the same time that nonwhites were becoming a much larger part of the Democratic electoral coalition, white southerners were leaving it.

Among white southerners, over these three decades, a 55-point Democratic advantage in party identification turned into a two-point Republican advantage: among all southern white voters in the 1984–1988 elections, Republicans outnumbered Democrats by

46 percent to 44 percent. Moreover, there was a large generational divide. Among white southerners aged forty-five and older, Democrats outnumbered Republicans by 52 percent to 38 percent. However, among those under forty-five, Republicans outnumbered Democrats by 53 percent to 37 percent. This age gap made the realignment of the white South almost certain to continue.

Between the 1952–1960 elections and the 1984–1988 elections, the southern white share of Democratic voters in the nation fell from 24 percent to 16 percent, while the nonwhite share rose from 7 percent to 29 percent. In the 1952–1960 elections, white southerners outnumbered nonwhites among Democratic voters by more than a three-to-one margin; among Democratic voters in the 1984–1988 elections, nonwhites outnumbered white southerners by nearly two to one. The consequences of this shift for Democratic Party leaders and candidates would eventually be profound. A combination of demographic shifts in the voting-age population and secular realignment within the electorate meant that the influence of the most conservative element of the Democratic coalition was clearly waning, while the influence of the most progressive element, at least on racial and social welfare issues, was growing.

The consequences of secular realignment become even more apparent when we break down the shifts in white voters' party identification by ideology between 1972 and 1988, among all white voters in general and among northern and southern white voters in particular. We begin in 1972 because the ANES survey of that year was the first one to ask about ideological identification. The shifts in party identification among white voters over this sixteen-year period were strongly related to ideology (table 2.8). Among both northern and southern whites, Republican gains were concentrated very heavily among self-identified conservatives. The change was especially dramatic among conservative southern whites: in 1972, they favored the Democratic Party by a five-point margin, but by

TABLE 2.8. CHANGE IN PARTY IDENTIFICATION OF IDEOLOGICAL GROUPS
AMONG WHITE VOTERS, 1972–1988

| Group | % Dem–% Rep | | |
	1972	1988	Change
All white voters	+ 5	– 13	– 18
Liberal	+ 43	+ 61	+ 18
Moderate (or no answer)	+ 13	+ 5	– 8
Conservative	– 29	– 57	– 28
Northern whites	– 1	– 16	– 15
Liberal	+ 43	+ 61	+ 18
Moderate (or no answer)	+ 5	– 1	– 6
Conservative	– 40	– 62	– 22
Southern whites	+ 28	– 3	– 31
Liberal	+ 44	+ 65	+ 21
Moderate (or no answer)	+ 42	+ 23	– 19
Conservative	+ 5	– 41	– 46

Source: ANES Cumulative File

1988, they favored the Republicans by 41 points. The shift among northern white conservatives was smaller because they were already solidly in the GOP camp in 1972. Nevertheless, the Republican advantage among this group grew from 40 points to 62 points over these sixteen years.

These figures show that while conservative whites were moving decisively toward the Republican Party, moderate whites shifted in the same direction, but much less dramatically. What really stands out, though, is that liberal whites in both North and South were moving in the opposite direction. Among liberal northern whites, the Democratic advantage in party identification grew from 43 points to 61 points, and among liberal southern whites, it grew from 44 points to 65 points. The result of these shifts was that the relationship between ideology and party identification was considerably stronger in 1988 than in 1972, especially in the South. In terms of shared variance, the relationship between ideology and party identification was about twice as strong in 1988 as in 1972 among northern whites, but about seven times as strong among southern whites.

As the Democratic Party grew increasingly dependent on votes from nonwhites during the 1970s and 1980s, large numbers of white voters fled to the GOP. This white flight had a clear ideological component: it was heavily concentrated among conservatives. This shift occurred in both the North and the South, but it was especially dramatic in the South because the residual loyalty of many conservative whites there meant that the party had more of them to lose.

As late as 1972, eight years after Lyndon Johnson's election on a pro–civil rights platform and seven years after the passage of the Voting Rights Act, the large majority of southern white voters and a plurality of southern white conservatives still identified with the Democratic Party. By 1988, however, a plurality of all southern white voters and the large majority of southern white conservatives had abandoned their parents' and grandparents' party and moved into the Republican camp. However, even as the Republican presidential candidate, George Bush of Texas, swept every southern state in 1988, Democrats retained an overwhelming majority of U.S. House and Senate seats along with every governorship, every state legislative chamber, and almost every state and local elected office in the South. Democratic dominance of southern congressional seats was the key to their control of the House and Senate. For that dominance to end, Republicans had to develop a strategy for converting their advantages in party identification and presidential voting into victories below the presidential level. They had to find a way to nationalize down-ballot elections. Starting in 1994, they did just that.

THREE

From Dealignment to Alignment

By the end of the 1980s, the electoral coalition forged by Franklin D. Roosevelt had largely collapsed. The Democratic advantage in party identification had shrunk to its smallest size since the American National Election Study began measuring party identification in 1952. Moreover, the Democrats' sharpest declines had occurred in the key components of the Roosevelt coalition: white southerners, northern white Catholics, and northern white blue-collar voters. By 1988, Republicans outnumbered Democrats among southern white voters and northern white blue-collar voters, and Democrats had only a slight advantage among northern white Catholic voters.

Having lost five of six presidential elections between 1968 and 1988 along with their advantage in party identification, the Democrats clearly were no longer the dominant party in American politics. However, while the Democrats had lost their position, the Republicans had not achieved anything approaching dominance either. Throughout the 1980s, Democrats continued to hold large majorities in the House of Representatives, and after a six-year interlude of GOP control, they regained control of the Senate in the 1986 midterm election and maintained that majority for the next eight years. They continued to control the large majority of the nation's governorships and state legislative chambers throughout the 1980s.

Rather than realignment, the 1970s and 1980s were a period of dealignment.[1] The large majority of voters continued to identify with one of the two major parties, but party loyalty in elections fell to its lowest levels since the ANES began in the 1950s. Ticket splitting was at an all-time high. Democratic voters regularly deserted their party's presidential candidates, while Republican voters crossed party lines in droves to support Democratic House and Senate candidates. Between 1972 and 1988 an average of 25 percent of voters split their presidential and House ballots, and 23 percent split their presidential and Senate ballots.[2] There was a clear asymmetry to their choices: far more voters chose a Republican presidential candidate and a Democratic House or Senate candidate than the reverse.

The frequent result of this pattern of ticket splitting was divided government in Washington.[3] During the twenty years between 1973 and 1993, there were only four years of unified Democratic control of Congress and the presidency, compared with sixteen years in which Republicans controlled the White House and Democrats controlled one or both chambers of Congress. No Republican president during this era had a completely Republican-controlled Congress to work with. Ronald Reagan did have a Republican Senate during six of his eight years in office, but even with his landslide reelection in 1984, Reagan could not break the Democrats' grip on the House.

The Partisan Revival Begins

The 1988 and 1992 elections gave little hint that the era of party dealignment was coming to an end. In 1992, Arkansas governor Bill Clinton became the first Democrat to win a presidential election since Jimmy Carter in 1976. Clinton's victory, however, in a three-way race with the Republican incumbent George Bush and the independent Ross Perot, hardly seemed like a transformational event.[4] Clinton ran as an ideological moderate, and his electoral coalition was not very different from Carter's—another southern governor and ideological moderate. Like Carter, Clinton came very close to winning the white vote, and he ran strongly in the South, carrying North Carolina, Tennessee, Georgia, Florida, and Louisiana along with his home state of Arkansas. Over the next two decades, however, demographic and cultural changes in American society would pave the way for a dramatic transformation of the American party system.

Although it was not obvious at the time, the signs of realignment were already evident by 1992. Bill Clinton did much better with traditional Democratic voting groups such as white southerners, northern white Catholics, and northern white blue-collar voters than the liberal northern Democrats Walter Mondale and Michael Dukakis had done in 1984 and '88. But his victory hardly represented a restoration of the old New Deal coalition. For one thing, a plurality of southern whites voted for Bush in 1992. Moreover, Clinton's victory did nothing to stem Republican gains in party identification among these traditionally Democratic voting groups.

The clearest indication that the era of dealignment was ending came not in a presidential election but in the 1994 midterms. Midterm elections almost always bring losses for the president's party in Congress, but what happened in 1994 went far beyond the typical pattern. The Democrats lost fifty-four seats in the House of Representatives and eight seats in the Senate, giving Republicans complete control of Congress for the first time in forty years. Moreover, the voting patterns in 1994 suggested that the GOP sweep was not merely a response to short-term forces such as discontent with the president's job performance. Rather, Republican gains reflected a successful effort by a group of younger House Republicans, led by minority whip Newt Gingrich of Georgia, to nationalize the congressional elections.[5]

Under the strategy developed by Gingrich and his allies, Republican candidates across the country focused on a common set of issues and common lines of attack against the Democratic president and Congress. Republican voters responded to this unified message with a sharp increase in party loyalty. Their defection rates fell from an average of 30 percent in the 1988–1992 House elections to only 17 percent in the 1994 House election, and from an average of 27 percent in the 1988–1992 Senate elections to only 16 percent in the 1994 Senate elections. These loyalty gains were especially marked in races involving Democratic incumbents. In these contests, Republican defection rates fell from an average of 50 percent in the 1988–1992 House elections to only 29 percent in the 1994 House elections, and from an average of 42 percent in the 1988–1992 Senate elections to only 24 percent in the 1994 Senate elections.

The increased loyalty of Republican voters gave the party major gains in districts and states that had long favored the GOP in presidential elections while electing Democrats to the House and Senate. Of the fifty-four seats picked up by Republicans in the House of Representatives, forty-one were in districts that were more Republican than the nation in the 1992 presidential election. While the pattern was less clear in the Senate elections, five of the eight seats picked up by Republicans were in states that were more Republican than the nation in 1992.

Race and Realignment

The 1994 elections reflected a gradual shift in the relative size of the Democratic and Republican electoral coalitions during the 1980s, a deliberate strategy by Republican leaders, and the normal tendency of voters to turn against the president's party in midterm elections. Nationalizing the 1994 election allowed Republicans to substantially increase their party identifiers' loyalty. However, the strategy worked only because of a gradual increase over two decades in Republican identification among traditionally Democratic voting groups.

There was a sharp increase in Republican identification among white voters between the election of Jimmy Carter in 1976 and the Reagan and Bush victories between 1980 and '88 (figure 3.1). During the 1980s, for the first time in the history of the ANES and probably for the first time since 1932, Republican identifiers outnumbered Democratic identifiers among white voters. The Republican advantage would continue to grow during the Clinton, George W. Bush, and Obama eras. By 2012, 55 percent of white voters identified with or leaned toward the GOP, while only 39 percent identified with or leaned toward the Democrats.

Growing Republican identification among white voters meant that the Democratic Party was becoming increasingly dependent on the support of African-Americans and other nonwhite voters. The trend in the racial composition of Democratic and Republican voters in presidential elections between 1976 and 2012 shows a marked increase for Democrats, and very little growth for Republicans (figure 3.2). Although the figure shows presidential elections only, the trend was very similar in midterm elections, even though the nonwhite share of the electorate was typically somewhat smaller. These data show that the dramatic racial divide between the Democratic and Republican electorates grew even faster after 1992. While

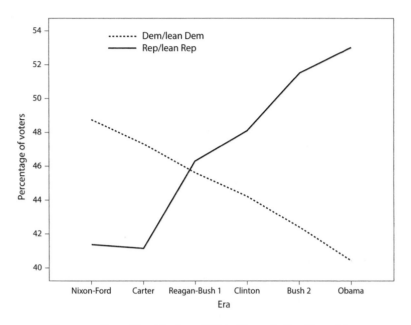

Figure 3.1. Party Identification of White Voters by Presidential Era.
Source: ANES Cumulative File

the nonwhite share of Democratic voters grew from 16 percent in 1976 to 45 percent in 2012, the nonwhite share of Republican voters only increased from 4 percent in 1976 to 10 percent in 2012. It actually declined slightly between 2004 and 2012.

These trends in Republican identification by white voters and Democratic voting by nonwhites reflect the responses of white and black voters to the changing positions of the national Democratic and Republican parties on racial and economic issues. Between the 1960s and the 1980s, Democratic presidential candidates from Lyndon Johnson and Hubert Humphrey to Walter Mondale and Michael Dukakis championed civil rights legislation and social welfare programs to combat racial and economic inequality, while Republican presidential candidates from Barry Goldwater and Richard

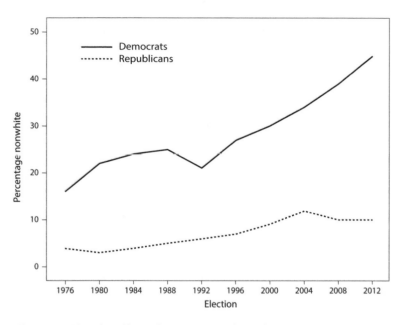

Figure 3.2. Nonwhite Share of Democratic and Republican Voters, 1976–2012.
Source: National Exit Polls

Nixon to Ronald Reagan and George H. W. Bush courted racially and economically conservative white voters with subtle and not-so-subtle appeals to racial fears and prejudice, and with opposition to social welfare programs that many working-class whites increasingly saw as primarily benefiting nonwhites.[6]

The trends in voting by nonwhites also reflect another development, whose effects became evident during the 1990s: the increasing racial diversity of American society. Since the 1980s, large-scale immigration from Latin America and Asia and higher birth rates among nonwhites have led to a dramatic increase in the nonwhite share of the American population and, more gradually, the nonwhite share of the American electorate. This growth is expected to continue for many years, and since most of the increase in the nonwhite share of the U.S. population is projected to come from natural increase rather than immigration, changes in immigration policy are unlikely to affect it. Since 2010, the majority of the infants born in the United States have been nonwhite. By the 2040s, the Census Bureau projects that non-Hispanic whites will be a minority of the population, although it will probably take another decade or two before they are a minority of the electorate.

The political consequences of what demographer William Frey has called a "diversity explosion" have already been profound.[7] There is little doubt, for example, that the nation's first African-American president, Barack Obama, could never have been nominated by the Democratic Party, let alone elected, if the nonwhite share of the U.S. electorate had not doubled between 1992 and 2008. Obama's reelection in 2012 clearly would not have happened without the overwhelming support of nonwhite voters, who made up a record 28 percent of the electorate that year. Despite losing the white vote by 20 percentage points in 2012—a record for any successful Democratic presidential candidate—Obama won more than 80 percent of the nonwhite vote, defeating his Republican challenger by almost 4 percentage points.

The widening of the racial divide between the Democratic and Republican electorates since the 1980s—a divide evident among the parties' candidates and elected representatives at all levels of government—has reflected two mutually reinforcing trends: a continued overwhelming Democratic advantage in party identification in the growing nonwhite share of the voting population, and a growing Republican advantage in party identification in the shrinking white share. The increase in Republican identification among white voters, however, was unevenly distributed across the white electorate. It was heavily concentrated among racial and economic conservatives: those whites most likely to be disturbed by the growing liberalism of the national Democratic Party and by the growing

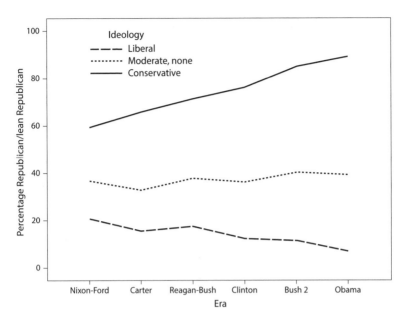

Figure 3.3. Republican Identification Among White Voters by Ideology and Presidential Era. Source: ANES Cumulative File

visibility and influence of African-Americans and other nonwhites within the party.

If we look at the trends in Republican identification among white voters between the Nixon-Ford era and the Obama era based on self-declared ideology, we can see that the increase in Republican identification among white voters was concentrated almost entirely among self-identified conservatives (figure 3.3). Over these four decades, Republican identification grew by more than 30 percentage points among conservative white voters, going from 60 percent in 1972 to 92 percent in 2012. During the same time period, Republican identification held steady among white voters who identified as moderates or had no clear ideological identification, going from 38 percent in 1972 to 42 percent in 2012. Moreover, it declined by

20 percentage points among white liberals, falling from 24 percent in 1972 to only 4 percent in 2012. These trends make it clear that the dramatic shift in the positions of the national Democratic and Republican parties on racial issues, and the growing visibility and influence of African-Americans and other nonwhites within the Democratic Party, created an ideological realignment among white voters.

Because of the growing relationship between ideology and party identification, the distance between white Democrats and white Republicans on the seven-point liberal-conservative scale almost tripled between 1972 and 2012. The average position of Democratic identifiers and leaners went from 3.9 to 3.2, and the average position of Republican identifiers and leaners moved from 4.6 to 5.2. To put this change in perspective, between 1972 and 2012 the proportion of self-identified liberals among white Democrats grew from 27 percent to 51 percent and the proportion of self-identified conservatives fell from 22 percent to 6 percent; meanwhile, the proportion of self-identified conservatives among white Republicans grew from 46 percent to 71 percent as the proportion of self-identified liberals fell from 11 percent to 1 percent and moderates from 43 percent to 28 percent. White Democrats were much more liberal in 2012 than in 1972, while white Republicans were more conservative.

Religion and Realignment

Race was certainly not the only factor pulling the Democratic and Republican electoral coalitions apart. Another major new divide within the electorate was religion and the cultural values associated with it. Religion has always been an important part of American life and culture, and even in the twenty-first century Americans remain far more religious than citizens of other major western industrialized democracies. Still, since the 1960s, American society and culture have grown increasingly secular. The past fifty years have seen dramatic changes in the role of women in American society, increased availability of modern methods of birth control, legalization of abortion, growing acceptance of premarital sex, divorce, and homosexual relationships including same-sex marriage, a gradual decline in the proportion of Americans identifying as Christians, and a gradual increase in the proportion with no religious affiliation.[8]

These changes are far-reaching, but they are far from universally accepted. Many Americans, especially evangelical Protestants and devout Catholics, remain adamantly opposed to these developments and have mounted a strong counter-movement in support of what religious conservatives call "traditional family values." Since the 1980s, organizations like the Christian Coalition and the Moral Majority have sought to elect public officials sympathetic to traditional values and to promote them through government policies, such as restrictions on access to abortion and bans on same-sex marriage. Women's rights, gay rights, and other liberal groups have in turn fought back. While the term "culture wars" is overused, it is clear that divisions over cultural issues have become much more prominent and have had a big impact on party politics.[9]

Since 1980, when the Republican Party first adopted a plank in its national platform calling for the repeal of the Supreme Court's *Roe v. Wade* decision legalizing abortion during the first trimester of pregnancy, the divide between Democrats and Republicans over cultural issues has been growing. Seeing an opportunity to win over a large bloc of previously Democratic or uncommitted voters, Republican leaders starting with Ronald Reagan have aggressively courted white religious conservatives. Democratic leaders have responded by pursuing the support of college-educated, secular, and culturally liberal voters. The result has been a growing religious divide between Republican and Democratic voters—primarily, however, among white voters. African-American and (to a lesser extent)

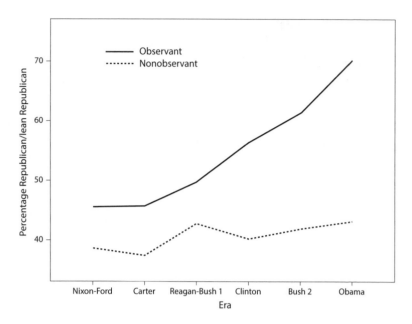

Figure 3.4. Party Identification of White Voters by Religious Observance and
Presidential Era. Source: ANES Cumulative File

Hispanic voters have been less attuned to cultural issues and more
focused on social welfare and economic issues.

The increasing religious divide can be seen clearly in the trends
in Republican identification among observant and nonobservant
white voters between 1972 and 2012 (figure 3.4). Voters were classified as "observant" if they reported attending religious services
either every week or almost every week, and as "nonobservant" if
they attended services only occasionally or never. These two groups
together accounted for close to 90 percent of white voters. (The
remaining 10 percent reported attending religious services "once
or twice a month." For greater clarity, this group, which saw a modest increase in Republican identification, is excluded from the ac-
companying figure.)

The data show that the partisan divide between observant and nonobservant white voters widened dramatically over these four decades, with most of the increase occurring after 1988. Among nonobservant whites, Republican identification remained almost flat between the Reagan–George H. W. Bush era and the Obama era. In 2012, Democratic identifiers and leaners continued to outnumber Republican identifiers and leaners in this group by 48 percent to 46 percent. However, there was a sharp increase in Republican identification among observant whites: by 2012, Republican identifiers and leaners outnumbered Democrats in this group, 72 percent to 25 percent. The results were similar in 2016. According to the ANES survey, Republican identifiers and leaners outnumbered Democratic identifiers and leaners by 68 percent to 26 percent among observant white voters. In contrast, among nonobservant white voters, Democratic identifiers and leaners outnumbered Republican identifiers and leaners by 51 percent to 39 percent.

The growing prominence of cultural issues powerfully affected many religious white voters. Data from the ANES surveys show that the growing visibility of the culture wars in election campaigns and the media tended to politicize traditional religious beliefs and values: Americans who supported these values increasingly came to see themselves as politically conservative. This effect is clearly evident if we examine the trends in ideological identification among observant and nonobservant white voters between 1972 and 2012 (figure 3.5). There was a sharp increase in the proportion of observant whites who considered themselves conservatives during the elections of the Clinton era (1992–1996), and this trend continued through the George W. Bush and Obama eras.

The increase in conservative ideological identification among observant white voters after 1988 was significant politically because of the growing connection between ideology and party identification among white voters during these years. This connection was

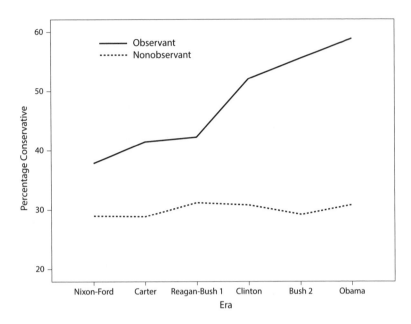

Figure 3.5. Ideology of White Voters by Religious Observance and Presidential Era. Source: ANES Cumulative File

stronger among observant whites than among nonobservant whites, and it increased sharply between the Reagan–George H. W. Bush era and the Obama era (table 3.1). In terms of shared variance, the relationship was about two times stronger among nonobservant whites during the Obama era than during the Reagan–George H. W. Bush era, but almost three times stronger among observant whites.

Taken together, the trends shown in figure 3.5 and table 3.1 tell us that since the 1970s, religious whites have become increasingly likely to identify as conservatives, and religious whites who consider themselves conservatives have become increasingly likely to identify as Republican. In 1972, only 38 percent of observant white voters considered themselves conservatives and only 58 percent of these religious conservatives identified with or leaned toward the

Table 3.1. Correlation of Ideology with Party Identification by Presidential Era Among Observant and Nonobservant White Voters

Presidential era	Observant	Nonobservant
Nixon-Ford	.265	.333
Carter	.351	.404
Reagan-Bush 1	.409	.457
Clinton	.544	.528
Bush 2	.588	.585
Obama	.688	.663

Source: ANES Cumulative File

Republican Party. By 2012, 59 percent of observant white voters considered themselves conservatives and 93 percent of these identified with or leaned toward the Republican Party. As a result of these trends, in the twenty-first century, white religious conservatives have become a major force in the Republican Party at the same time that culturally liberal, secular whites were becoming a major force in the Democratic Party.

Ideological Polarization, Negative Partisanship, and Party Loyalty

Democratic and Republican political leaders have responded very differently to growing racial and religious divisions in American society. Since the 1960s, Democratic leaders have increasingly embraced the cause of civil rights and racial equality, while Republican leaders have taken positions intended to appeal to racially conservative white voters. They have opposed "special rights" for minorities and supported voter identification laws and other policies restricting access to the polls that disproportionately affect nonwhite voters. On newer cultural issues that have arisen since the 1980s such as LGBT rights and access to abortion, Democratic leaders have increasingly adopted liberal positions designed to appeal to unmarried women, gays, and younger, mostly college-educated secular white voters, while Republican leaders have increasingly taken positions that appeal to older, religious white voters. The result has been a growing racial, religious, and ideological divide between the electoral bases of the two major parties. In the twenty-first century, to a large and growing degree, the Democrats have become the party of nonwhites and white liberals while the Republicans have become the party of white conservatives.

As the parties have moved apart, supporters of each party have come to perceive a widening gap between their policy preferences and the policies advocated by the opposing party. Evidence of this growing gap can be seen by plotting in graph form the average perceived distance of Democratic and Republican identifiers and leaners from their own party and the opposing party on the seven-point liberal scale. Over four decades from the Nixon-Ford era to the Obama era, the average perceived distance of partisans from their own party has remained almost constant, just over one unit out of a maximum of six (figure 3.6). Over the same period, however, partisans' average perceived distance from the opposing party has increased from just over two units to almost 3.5.

Compared with thirty or forty years ago, far fewer partisans today perceive the opposing party as relatively close ideologically, and far more see it as very distant. In 1972, 46 percent of partisans placed the opposing party within one unit of themselves on the seven-point ideology scale, while only 15 percent placed the opposing party four or more units away from themselves. However, by 2012, just 16 percent placed the opposing party within one unit of themselves, versus 45 percent who placed it four or more units away.

This increase in perceived distance from the opposing party is significant because ideological proximity is strongly related to both partisan affect and voting behavior: partisans who perceive the opposing party as relatively close ideologically are much more likely

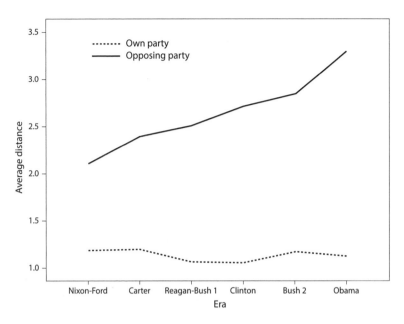

Figure 3.6. Average Perceived Ideological Distance from Own Party and Opposing Party by Presidential Era. Source: ANES Cumulative File

to have positive feelings toward it and to consider voting for its candidates. In 2012, among the 10 percent of partisans who placed the opposing party within one unit of themselves on the ideology scale, that party's average rating on the feeling thermometer was 44 degrees and the level of consistent loyalty only 65 percent. Meanwhile, the 48 percent of partisans who placed the opposing party at least four units away from themselves gave that party an average rating of only 22 degrees, and the level of consistent loyalty was 88 percent.

As the racial, cultural, and ideological divides between the two major parties have widened, Democratic and Republican voters have become increasingly negative about the opposing party and its leaders. Between 1978, the first year in which the ANES survey

TABLE 3.2. RATINGS OF OPPOSING PARTY ON FEELING
THERMOMETER BY PRESIDENTIAL ERA

Presidential era	Positive	Neutral	Negative	Total
Carter	31	32	37	100
Reagan-Bush 1	32	23	45	100
Clinton	24	18	58	100
Bush 2	21	19	60	100
Obama	13	17	70	100

Note: Read percentages horizontally.

Source: ANES Cumulative File

asked respondents to rate the parties on the feeling thermometer, and 2012, partisans' average rating of the opposing party fell from 47 degrees to 30. Between 1968, the first year the ANES survey used the feeling thermometer scale, and 2012, partisans' average rating of the opposing party's presidential candidate fell from 54 degrees to 29.

Far more Democratic and Republican voters have negative feelings about the opposing party and its leaders today than they did in the past. We can see how significant this change has been if we look at the proportions of partisans who gave the opposing party a rating that was positive (above 50 degrees), neutral (50 degrees), or negative (below 50 degrees) during every presidential era from Carter through Obama. The change in these feelings over these four decades has been dramatic (table 3.2). In 1976, 63 percent of partisans gave the opposing party a positive or neutral rating and only 37 percent gave it a negative rating. During the Obama elections of 2008–2012, only 30 percent of partisans gave the opposing party a positive or neutral rating; 70 percent were negative.

This change has contributed to the most important trend in Americans' voting behavior over the past three decades—a dramatic increase in party loyalty and straight-ticket voting. Partisans who

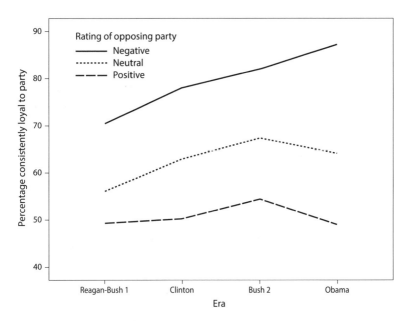

Figure 3.7. Party Loyalty by Rating of Opposing Party on Feeling Thermometer by Presidential Era. Source: ANES Cumulative File

dislike the opposing party are much more likely to cast a straight party ballot. This difference can be seen very clearly by graphing the trends in consistent party loyalty between the Reagan–George H. W. Bush era and the Obama era among partisans who rated the opposing party on the feeling thermometer (figure 3.7).

Throughout this period, those who had negative feelings toward the opposing party were much more loyal than those with neutral or positive feelings. Also, however, there was a much greater increase in party loyalty among those with negative feelings than among the other two groups. In 2012, 87 percent of partisans with negative feelings toward the opposing party voted consistently for their own party's candidates, compared with 68 percent of partisans with neutral feelings and only 52 percent of those with positive feelings.

Nationalization of House and Senate Elections

If the rise of negative partisanship has brought a substantial increase in party loyalty and straight-ticket voting, common sense
tells us that this should show up in House and Senate elections—
and it does. Growing party loyalty and straight-ticket voting have
produced a dramatic increase in the connection between presidential and House elections since the 1970s: the correlation between
the Democratic share of the House vote and the Democratic share
of the presidential vote in districts with contested races averaged
.54 between 1972 and 1980, .65 between 1982 and 1990, .78 between 1992 and 2000, .83 between 2002 and 2010, and .94 in 2012–
2014. In terms of shared variance, the relationship between presidential and House elections is now three times stronger than it was
in the 1970s.

These results show that the determinants of House election outcomes have changed, and that the relative importance of district
presidential partisanship is increasing at the expense of more local
factors, especially the advantage of incumbency. To test this hypothesis, and to measure changes in the relative influence of presidential partisanship and incumbency on the outcomes of individual House races over time, I conducted regression analyses of the
outcome of every House election between 1972 and 2014. The
dependent variable in these analyses is the Democratic percentage
of the major-party vote; the independent variables are the Democratic share of the major-party presidential vote in each district in
relation to the nation, and the party of the House incumbent, coded
as +1 for contests with Democratic incumbents, 0 for open seat
contests, and –1 for contests with Republican incumbents.

There were drastic changes in the effects of the two independent
variables during the five decades included in my analysis (table 3.3).
The overall explanatory power of the model increased substantially
over time, but this increase was entirely due to the influence of

TABLE 3.3. RESULTS OF REGRESSION ANALYSES OF HOUSE ELECTION OUTCOMES, 1972–2014

Year	Unstandardized coefficients		R square
	Presidential partisanship	Party of incumbent	
1972	.434	13.7	.77
1974	.316	12.6	.70
1976	.712	11.9	.76
1978	.638	12.9	.74
1980	.656	13.1	.79
1982	.649	11.5	.78
1984	.614	13.1	.86
1986	.479	15.4	.83
1988	.519	15.4	.86
1990	.424	11.6	.75
1992	.636	9.9	.75
1994	.674	10.6	.83
1996	.726	9.4	.86
1998	.702	10.9	.87
2000	.631	12.1	.89
2002	.572	12.6	.89
2004	.626	11.3	.92
2006	.626	10.2	.85
2008	.649	9.6	.89
2010	.848	6.6	.88
2012	.854	4.9	.94
2014	.828	4.9	.92
Avg. 1972–1980	.551	12.8	.75
Avg. 1982–1990	.537	13.4	.82
Avg. 1992–2000	.674	10.6	.84
Avg. 2002–2010	.664	10.1	.89
Avg. 2012–2014	.841	4.9	.93

Note: Dependent variable is percentage of major-party vote for Democratic House candidate in contested races. Estimates for intercepts not shown. All estimated coefficients are statistically significant at the .001 level based on one-tailed t-tests.

Sources: Gary Jacobson and data compiled by author

district partisanship. This influence increased considerably over time, with the largest increase occurring during the most recent time period. The effect of incumbency decreased slightly during the 1990s and 2000s and then dropped dramatically during the Obama years. Over these twenty-two elections, the three in which presidential partisanship was most important, as well as the three in which incumbency was least important, were the three most recent elections. Compared with the 1970s and 1980s, the electoral fortunes of House incumbents now depend much less on how effectively they cultivate their constituencies and much more on those constituencies' partisan makeup. To an ever greater extent, people vote for the party, not the person.

These results demonstrate that House elections have become increasingly nationalized. The outcomes of House elections are now determined to a much greater degree by the relative popularity within each House district of the Democratic and Republican presidential candidates. This shift is readily apparent in trends in the percentage of House contests won by Democrats and Republicans in House districts that favor each party based on the results of presidential elections. The favored presidential party is determined here by the Democratic share of the major-party presidential vote in the district compared with the nation. A district where the Democratic presidential candidate wins a greater share of the vote than he or she did in the nation as a whole is considered a Democratic-leaning district, while a district where the Democratic candidate won a smaller percentage than he or she did nationally is considered a Republican-leaning district.[10]

Since 1990, there has been a sharp increase in the proportion of House contests won by the candidate of the favored presidential party, but this increase has been much greater in Republican-leaning districts than in Democratic-leaning districts (figure 3.8). Between the 1960s and the 1980s, Republicans won fewer than 60 percent of

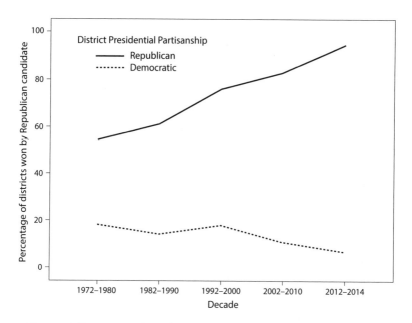

Figure 3.8. Percentage of Republican House Winners by District Presidential Party Advantage by Decade. Sources: Gary Jacobson and data compiled by author

House races in districts that were more Republican than the nation in presidential elections, at a time when Democrats were winning about 80 percent of House races that were more Democratic than the nation in presidential elections. Since 1994, however, and especially since 2010, GOP candidates have enjoyed much more success in Republican-leaning districts. This improvement in Republican fortunes is directly related to the increasing connection between presidential and House voting.

In the most recent time period, 2012–2014, the relationship between presidential and House voting has been very strong. In these elections, Republicans have won 95 percent of contests in Republican-leaning districts, while Democrats have won 93 percent of contests in Democratic-leaning districts. This pattern of strong partisan consistency favors Republicans because more districts lean Republican than lean Democratic. This difference is not new. Republicans have long enjoyed an advantage in House elections because Democratic voters are inefficiently distributed across House districts. What has changed in recent years is not the proportion of Republican-leaning districts but the Republicans' ability to convert their advantage in district presidential partisanship into actual majorities of House seats. This change is directly attributable to the nationalization of House elections.

Senate elections have also become increasingly nationalized because of growing party loyalty and straight-ticket voting. The trend there has been very similar to the trend in House elections, but even more dramatic because the connection between presidential and Senate elections used to be considerably weaker than the connection between presidential and House elections. The average correlation between the Democratic share of the presidential vote and the Democratic share of the Senate vote in states with contested races has risen from .16 between 1972 and 1980 to .25 between 1982 and 1990, .42 between 1992 and 2000, .66 between 2002 and 2010, and .84 in 2012–2014. In terms of shared variance, the relationship is now more than four times stronger than it was in the 1990s and twenty-five times stronger than it was in the 1970s.

As with House elections, these results show that the relative importance of presidential partisanship in Senate elections has been increasing at the expense of more local factors, especially the advantage of incumbency. As I did with House races, I conducted regression analyses of the outcomes of Senate elections for each decade since the 1970s. I combined Senate elections by decade because of the relatively small number of Senate contests in each election year. As with House elections, the dependent variable in these analyses is the Democratic percentage of the major-party vote in contested races.

TABLE 3.4. RESULTS OF REGRESSION ANALYSES OF
SENATE ELECTION OUTCOMES BY DECADE

| | Unstandardized coefficients | | |
Decade	Presidential partisanship	Party of incumbent	R square
1972–1980	.395	6.5	.35
1982–1990	.362	10.0	.56
1992–2000	.461	9.5	.59
2002–2010	.602	9.2	.71
2012–2014	.683	6.1	.86

Note: Dependent variable is percentage of major-party vote for Democratic Senate candidate in contested races. Estimates for intercepts and election-year fixed effects not shown. All estimated coefficients are statistically significant at the .001 level based on one-tailed t-tests.

Sources: Data compiled by author

The independent variables in the Senate regression equations are the Democratic share of the major-party presidential vote in each state in relation to the nation, and the party of the incumbent, coded as +1 for contests with Democratic incumbents, 0 for open-seat contests, and –1 for contests with Republican incumbents.

The trends in Senate elections were very similar to those found in House elections. There were drastic changes in the effects of the two key independent variables over five decades (table 3.4). The effect of state presidential partisanship increased considerably over time, with the largest increases occurring during the past two decades, at the same time that the effect of incumbency declined dramatically. The electoral fortunes of Senate incumbents, like those of House incumbents, now depend less on their personal popularity and more on the partisan makeup of their states.

The nationalization of House and Senate elections has brought a sharp increase in consistency between the outcomes of these two types of elections. I classified states as Democratic-leaning or

Republican-leaning in the same way that I classified House districts. States in which the Democratic presidential candidate's share of the major-party vote was greater than his share of the national major-party vote were classified as Democratic-leaning, while those where his share was less than his share of the national major-party vote were classified as Republican-leaning. This allows us to measure the proportions of Senate contests won by the Democratic candidate in Democratic-leaning states and by the Republican candidate in Republican-leaning states over the past five decades.

Since the 1980s, there has been a dramatic increase in the proportion of Senate races won by the party with the advantage in the presidential vote (figure 3.9). This has occurred in both Democratic-leaning states and Republican-leaning states. Democratic-leaning states are now much more likely to elect Democratic senators than they were during the 1980s, and Republican-leaning states are much more likely to elect Republican senators. In 2014, thirty-three of thirty-six Senate contests were won by the candidate of the advantaged party: Democrats won twelve of fifteen contests in states that were more Democratic than the nation in the 2012 presidential election, while Republicans won all twenty-one contests in states that were more Republican than the nation in 2012.

Between the 1972–1980 elections and those of 2012–2014, both parties substantially improved their performance in states in which they were advantaged based on presidential election results. In each decade, however, Democratic candidates won a somewhat larger share of seats in Democratic-leaning states than Republican candidates won in Republican-leaning states. In the 2012–2014 elections, for example, Democratic candidates won 88 percent (thirty of thirty-four) of contests in Democratic-leaning states, while Republican candidates won 80 percent (twenty-eight of thirty-five) of contests in Republican-leaning states.

Until 2014, Democrats had fared better in Senate elections than

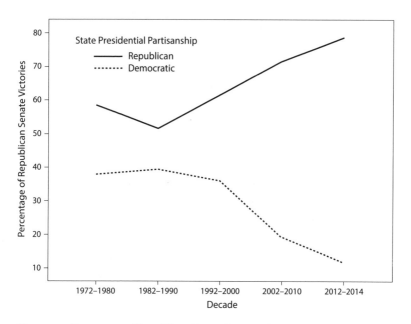

Figure 3.9. Percentage of Republican Senate Winners by State Presidential Party
Advantage by Decade. Source: Data compiled by author

in House elections because of their success in winning Senate contests in Republican-leaning states. The question now is whether,
given the increasing nationalization of Senate elections, they can
continue winning such contests in the future. If they cannot, the
Republican advantage in House elections may be joined by a similar advantage in Senate elections.

Nationalization of State Legislative Elections

The rise of negative partisanship also affects elections for state and
local offices. Party loyalty and straight-ticket voting mean that
party strength in state legislatures now reflects the results of presidential elections much more closely than in earlier decades. In 2012,
the correlation between the Democratic share of the presidential

vote and the Democratic share of state legislative seats was .85—
the strongest correlation between these two variables for any election year since at least 1956. The average correlation increased from
.40 between 1972 and 1988 to .58 between 1992 and 2000, and to
.73 between 2004 and 2012.

The growing connection between presidential and state legislative elections has had a dramatic impact on party control of state
legislatures. In thirty-eight of the forty-nine states with partisan
state legislative elections, the same party that won the 2012 presidential election controlled both chambers of the legislature in 2013.
However, the Republicans had a substantial advantage in control of
state legislatures: they controlled both chambers in twenty-one
of twenty-three states carried by Mitt Romney, while Democrats
controlled both chambers in only seventeen of twenty-six states
carried by Barack Obama.

Republican success in state legislative elections has clearly been
aided by the inefficient distribution of Democratic voters across
legislative districts in many states and by Republican control of
redistricting in many states in the aftermath of the 2010 midterm
election, including several states that voted for Barack Obama in
both 2008 and 2012. But the main driver of Republican gains in state
legislatures in recent years has been the same transformation that
has worked for them in the U.S. House of Representatives—the
nationalization of elections as a result of growing partisan consistency in voting.

In the 1980s and 1990s, Democrats controlled many legislative
chambers in states that regularly voted for Republican presidential
candidates, including many states in the South. As recently as 2001,
Democrats controlled twenty-four legislative chambers in the thirty
states carried by George W. Bush in the 2000 presidential election.
In the past decade, however, Republicans have taken control of
almost all of these chambers. In 2013, Democrats controlled only

three chambers in the twenty-four states carried by Mitt Romney in 2012. The growing connection between presidential and state legislative elections means that the divide between state politics and national politics, once very clear, has largely disappeared in much of the country.

The Electoral Consequences of Party Alignment

Since the 1980s, the two major parties' electoral bases have become increasingly aligned in response to growing racial, cultural, and ideological divisions in American society. Overlapping racial, cultural, and ideological divisions between the Democratic and Republican electorates have produced a system in which the large majority of partisans feel disdain, or worse, toward the opposing party and its leaders. The resulting high levels of party loyalty and straight-ticket voting have, in turn, produced a high degree of consistency between the outcomes of presidential and down-ballot elections.

Much more than at any recent time, the outcomes of House and Senate elections reflect the relative strength of the presidential parties in the House districts and states. This consistency between electoral outcomes is reinforced by another feature of the newly aligned party system: one-party domination of many geographic divisions, including most states and an overwhelming majority of House districts. The racial, cultural, and ideological realignment of the electorate has produced a dramatic geographic realignment of party strength—one that has little to do with partisan gerrymandering.

FOUR

The Changing Political Geography of the United States

The same trends that have dramatically altered the composition of the Democratic and Republican electoral coalitions have also produced major shifts in the parties' geographic bases. The map of each party's strongest support in presidential and congressional elections is very different from the map that prevailed during the first few decades after World War II. These shifts in the parties' geographic bases have had profound consequences for the conduct of American political campaigns and the distribution of political power in the country.

Just as the racial, cultural, and ideological divides between the parties have widened in recent decades, so has the geographic divide. As recently as the 1980s, geographic patterns of party support varied considerably from one presidential election to the next, depending on the candidates' regional identities and ideological orientations. Very few states could be considered safe for one party or the other. There was very little relationship, for instance, between the pattern of support for George McGovern, a strong liberal from

South Dakota, in 1972, and the pattern of support just four years later for Jimmy Carter, a moderate from Georgia. Across the fifty states and the District of Columbia, the correlation between the Democratic share of the vote in 1972 and that in 1976 was a very modest .44.

Meanwhile, in the House and Senate, the regional bases of the parties continued to reflect the patterns established during the 1930s and 1940s in the aftermath of the New Deal realignment, with Democrats dominant in the South and the large cities of the North. The results of presidential elections often bore little resemblance to the results of House and Senate elections. Since the 1990s, however, and especially since 2000, the parties' geographic bases have become far more stable between elections, and the relationship between presidential and congressional election outcomes has strengthened. This stability is a direct result of the past forty years' ideological realignment.

We can gain a sense of how the parties' geographic bases have changed by comparing the Electoral College coalition assembled by Barack Obama in 2008 with those of the two previous Democratic presidents in their initial elections: Jimmy Carter in 1976 and Bill Clinton in 1992. Obama's 2008 Electoral College coalition looks very little like Carter's and only somewhat like Clinton's.

A useful statistic for measuring the degree of consistency between the Electoral College coalitions across elections is the correlation between a party's vote share across the fifty states and the District of Columbia in the two contests. A correlation of one would indicate perfect consistency, while a correlation of zero would indicate no relationship at all. The correlation between Obama's vote share in 2008 and Clinton's in 1992 is only .73, and the correlation between Obama's vote share and Carter's in 1976 is a far weaker .41. This means that Obama's and Clinton's vote shares have only 52 percent of their variance in common, while Obama's and

Carter's have just 17 percent of their variance in common. Obama did very poorly in a number of states that Carter won handily, including Georgia, Arkansas, and West Virginia; but Obama did very well in a number of states that Carter lost in 1976, including New Jersey, Michigan, Illinois, and California.

In contrast, the correlation between Obama's vote share in 2008 and Democratic nominee John Kerry's in 2004 is a very strong .94, and the correlation between Obama's vote share in 2008 and Al Gore's in 2000 is almost as strong at .89. This means that Obama's and Kerry's vote shares have 89 percent of their variance in common, while Obama's and Gore's have 79 percent of their variance in common. In general, Obama, Kerry, and Gore ran strongly in the same states and did poorly in the same states.

Another way to compare the Democratic and Republican Electoral College coalitions in two elections is simply to count the number of states supporting the same party or different parties in each election. When we compare the 2008 and 1992 elections, we find that thirty-eight states and the District of Columbia supported the same party while twelve supported different parties; when we compare the 2008 and 1976 elections, only twenty-three states and the District of Columbia supported the same party while twenty-seven supported different parties. Once again, we see that Obama's Electoral College coalition had very little in common with Carter's coalition.

Perhaps the most politically significant difference between Carter's Electoral College coalition and both Clinton's and Obama's coalitions is the dramatic decline in the importance of the South and the Border South. Carter carried twenty-three states and the District of Columbia in 1976. Thirteen of those states were in the South or the Border South, and they provided 145 of his 297 electoral votes, or 49 percent of the total. Thus, the South was absolutely critical to Carter's victory. In 1992, however, despite his southern roots and his choice of fellow southerner Al Gore as his running mate, Bill Clinton carried only seven states in the South and Border South, and they provided only 63 of his 370 electoral votes, or 17 percent of the total. Barack Obama carried only three states in the South or Border South in 2008, and they provided only 55 of his 365 electoral votes, or 15 percent of the total. Both Obama and Clinton would have won the presidency with no help at all from the South and Border South.

Clinton and Obama more than made up for their lack of southern support by doing substantially better than Jimmy Carter in the Northeast, the industrial Midwest, and the Pacific Coast. Carter won only six of the eleven states in the Northeast, losing New Jersey, Connecticut, New Hampshire, Vermont, and Maine, whereas both Clinton and Obama won all eleven states in the region. In the industrial Midwest, Carter lost Illinois and Michigan, two states with large numbers of electoral votes; Clinton and Obama carried both states. In addition, Carter lost every Pacific Coast state except Hawaii, but Clinton and Obama easily carried Oregon, Washington, and California as well. Those victories in the Northeast, industrial Midwest, and Pacific Coast region were worth 144 electoral votes—more than half of the number that Clinton and Obama needed to win the presidency.

Ideological Realignment in the States

The difference between the group of states that voted for Jimmy Carter in 1976 and those that voted for Obama in 2008 reflects a dramatic change in the geographic bases of the two major parties. Carter won with an Electoral College coalition largely resembling that of Democratic presidential candidates of the 1950s and 1960s, one based largely in the South and Border South and including some large industrial states in the Northeast and Midwest. His Electoral College coalition was very similar to John F. Kennedy's coalition in 1960: thirty-nine of fifty states, along with the District of Columbia, supported the same party in the 1960 and 1976 presidential elections. In contrast, Barack Obama won the 2008 presidential election with an Electoral College coalition that was based in the Northeast, the industrial Midwest, and the Pacific Coast region. Carter's election can be seen as an echo of the old New Deal coalition; Obama's win, even more than Clinton's, marked the emergence of a new Democratic electoral coalition.

The changing geographic bases of the two parties can be seen very clearly in measures of the relationship between state party identification in 1974–1982 and state party identification in 2012. For both periods, state party identification is measured by the difference between the percentage of Democratic identifiers and the percentage of Republican identifiers, compared with the national average. States were given a positive score if they were more Democratic than the national average and a negative score if they were more Republican.[1]

The most striking thing about these measurements is the surprisingly weak relationship between state party strength in 1974–1982 and state party strength in 2012: the correlation between these two measures is just .26 (figure 4.1). Knowing a state's partisan leaning in the late 1970s gives one almost no ability to predict its partisan leaning in 2012. In fact, a number of states that tilted strongly Democratic during the earlier period were Republican strongholds by 2012, while several formerly competitive or Republican-leaning states had shifted to strongly Democratic.

The size of some of these swings is truly impressive. Alabama, for example, went from 21 points more Democratic than the nation to 17 points more Republican. Oklahoma went from 14 points more Democratic to 12 points more Republican. Meanwhile, Connecticut went from 4 points more Republican than the nation to 15 points more Democratic, and Vermont went from 14 points more

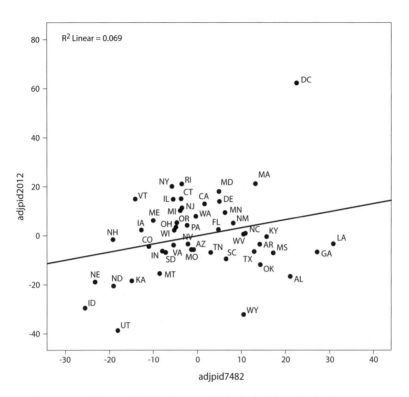

Figure 4.1. Geographic Realignment: State Party Identification in 2012 by State Party Identification in 1974–1982. Sources: For 1974–1982, CBS/New York Times polling data compiled by Wright, Erikson, and McIver; for 2012, Gallup Poll data.

Republican to 15 points more Democratic. Moreover, not all of the big movers were small states. Texas, now the nation's second most populous state, went from 13 points more Democratic than the nation to 7 points more Republican, while New York, now the nation's fourth most populous state, went from 6 points more Republican to 20 points more Democratic.

There was a clear regional pattern to these shifts in state partisanship, and in particular a major shift in party identification in the

TABLE 4.1. TRENDS IN STATE PARTY IDENTIFICATION BY REGION,
1974–1982 AND 2012

Region	Adjusted party ID 1974–1982	Adjusted party ID 2012	Change
South	+ 12.8	− 4.4	− 16.6
Northeast	− 1.7	+ 14.3	+ 16.0
Midwest	− 5.5	+ 3.3	+ 8.8
Mountain West	− 7.4	− 11.1	− 3.7
Pacific Coast	+ 1.0	+ 11.6	+ 10.6

Note: Entries shown are based on differences between percentages of Democratic and Republican identifiers in each state. Data are weighted by number of U.S. House districts in each state to reflect population. Party identification is measured in relation to national average.

Sources: For 1974–1982, CBS/New York Times polling data compiled by Wright, Erikson, and McIver; for 2012, Gallup Poll data.

South during this period (table 4.1). During the late 1970s and early '80s, the South was still the most Democratic region, but by 2012 it was more Republican than the rest of the nation. Only the sparsely populated Mountain West tilted more strongly toward the GOP.

While the South was trending strongly toward the Republican Party, there was an equally dramatic shift toward the Democratic Party in the Northeast and a somewhat smaller but still substantial shift in the same direction in the Pacific Coast region. Although both regions were close to the national average during the late 1970s and early '80s, by 2012 they were considerably more Democratic than the rest of the nation. Based on party identification data, by 2012 both the Northeast and the Pacific Coast states tilted more strongly toward the Democratic Party than the southern states tilted toward the Republican Party.

These regional patterns of partisan change suggest that shifts in party support between 1974–1982 and 2012 reflected the parties' ideological realignment. At the same time that states with relatively conservative electorates like Alabama, Texas, and Oklahoma were trending Republican, states with relatively liberal electorates like New York and California were trending Democratic. This can be shown in scatterplot graphs of the relationship between state ideology and partisanship in 1974–1982 and 2012.

The resulting patterns reflect a drastic change in the relationship between state ideology and partisanship between the two time periods (figure 4.2). In 1974–1982, there was essentially no relationship between state ideology and partisanship—the correlation between these two variables across the forty-seven states for which data were available (plus the District of Columbia) was a minuscule .03. Some of the most conservative states in the nation, including Mississippi, Oklahoma, South Carolina, and Texas, tilted strongly toward the Democratic Party in the 1970s, while some of the most liberal states in the nation, including California, New York, New Jersey, and Connecticut, were closely divided in party identification. Vermont, one of the most liberal states in the nation, was also one of the most Republican.

By 2012, however, there was a very strong relationship between state ideology and partisanship: the correlation between these two variables was .90. A quick glance at the data shows that by 2012, liberal states like New York, Massachusetts, Hawaii, and Connecticut all tilted strongly Democratic, while conservative states like Texas, South Carolina, Kansas, and Wyoming all tilted strongly Republican. States that were close to the national average on party identification, such as Florida, Ohio, Iowa, and Colorado, were also generally close to the national average on ideology.

The key question raised by the dramatic change in the relationship between state ideology and partisanship between 1982 and 2012 is what caused it. If we look at the correlations among four variables—state ideology in 1974–1982, state partisanship in 1974–1982, state ideology in 2012, and state partisanship in 2012—we

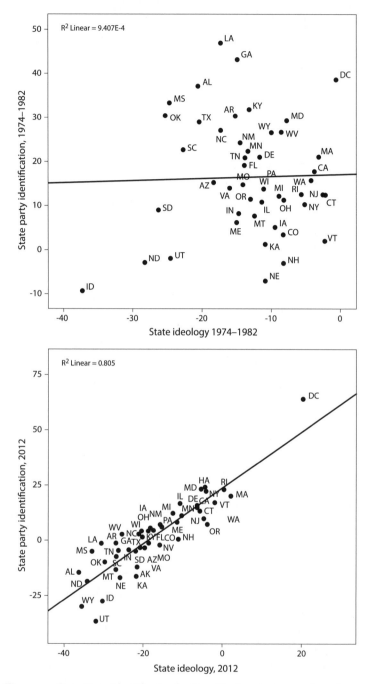

Figure 4.2. State Party Identification by State Ideology in 1974–1982 and 2012.
Sources: For 1974–1982, CBS/New York Times polling data compiled by
Wright, Erikson, and McIver; for 2012, Gallup Poll data.

TABLE 4.2. CORRELATIONS OF 1974–1982 STATE PARTISANSHIP AND IDEOLOGY
WITH 2012 STATE PARTISANSHIP AND IDEOLOGY

	1974–1982 PID	2012 PID	2012 IDEO
1974–1982 IDEO	.031	.684**	.734**
1974–1982 PID		.263*	−.042
2012 PID			.897**

Note: IDEO = ideology. PID = party identification. Entries shown are Pearson product-moment correlation coefficients. Coefficients marked with a single asterisk are significant at the .05 level. Coefficients marked with a double asterisk are significant at the .001 level. Significance levels based on one-tailed t-tests.

Sources: For 1974–1982, CBS/New York Times polling data compiled by Wright, Erikson, and McIver; for 2012, Gallup Poll data.

see, first, that although there is a very strong relationship between state ideology in 1974–1982 and state ideology in 2012, there is a very weak relationship between state partisanship in 1974–1982 and state partisanship in 2012 (table 4.2). Over these thirty-plus years, ideology was far more stable than partisanship. This finding runs counter to the traditional view that party identification is a very stable orientation at both the individual and aggregate levels.[2]

The other major finding that emerges from these figures is that there is a very strong relationship between state ideology in 1974–1982 and state partisanship in 2012 but almost no relationship, in fact a weak negative relationship, between state partisanship in 1974–1982 and state ideology in 2012. These results suggest that while state ideology in 1974–1982 had a substantial influence on state party identification in 2012, state party identification in 1974–1982 had little influence on state ideology in 2012. In other words, the dramatic change in the relationship between state ideology and party identification over these three decades came from an ideological realignment of party identification.

To test this hypothesis, I conducted a regression analysis of state party identification in 2012. The independent variables were state

TABLE 4.3. RESULTS OF REGRESSION ANALYSIS OF
2012 STATE PARTY IDENTIFICATION

Independent variable	B	Standard error	Beta	t-ratio	Sig.
PID7482	−.070	(.166)	−.056	−.423	N.S.
IDEO7482	1.424	(.203)	.664	7.025	.001
BLACK2010	.623	(.194)	.424	3.211	.002
HISPANIC2010	.177	(.161)	.106	1.100	N.S.

Notes: B = unstandardized regression coefficient. Beta = standardized regression coefficient. PID7482 = party identification, 1974–1982. IDEO7482 = ideology, 1974–1982. BLACK2010 = percentage African-American in 2010 Census. HISPANIC2010 = percentage Hispanic in 2010 Census. Intercept not shown. R-square = .62; adjusted R-square = .58. Significance levels based on one-tailed t-tests. N.S. = not statistically significant at .05 level.

Sources: For 1974–1982, CBS/New York Times polling data compiled by Wright, Erikson, and McIver; for 2012, Gallup Poll data; for black and Hispanic percentage of state population, 2010 Census data.

party identification in 1974–1982 and state ideology in 1974–1982, along with the African-American and Hispanic percentages of each state's population according to the 2010 Census (since one would expect states with larger African-American and Hispanic populations to be more Democratic).

These findings provide additional confirmation that the dramatic changes in party strength in the states between 1982 and 2012 were the products of an ideological realignment (table 4.3). The scope of this realignment is shown by the finding that state party strength in 1974–1982 had no effect at all on state party strength in 2012. In contrast, state ideology in 1974–1982 had a very strong impact on state party strength in 2012. According to these results, a one-percentage point increase in liberalism in 1974–1982 was associated with a 1.4 percentage point increase in Democratic strength in 2012.

The regression analysis shows that in addition to ideology, the size of a state's black population had a substantial impact on state party strength in 2012. An increase of one percentage point in the African-American share of the population in the 2010 Census was associated with a 0.6 percentage point increase in Democratic strength in 2012. A larger Hispanic population also moved a state toward the Democrats, but the difference was not statistically significant. Perhaps this is because Hispanic voters do not identify nearly as overwhelmingly with the Democratic Party as African-Americans do. Taken together, however, the analysis demonstrated here provides solid support for the argument that the American party system in the twenty-first century is based largely on ideology and race.

How Ideological Realignment Affects Election Outcomes

The realignment of party strength in the states has had profound consequences for election results. We can see this by looking at how state party identification and ideology correlate with the results of presidential elections in two different eras: 1972–1984 and 2000–2012. Each era includes four presidential elections.

There was a dramatic change in the pattern of relationships between presidential election results and both state party identification and state ideology (table 4.4). During the earlier era, these relationships were inconsistent, varying considerably from election to election depending on the candidates and major issues at stake. However, none of the correlations during this era were very strong. In 1972, when the liberal anti–Vietnam War crusader George McGovern was the Democratic presidential candidate, there was no relationship at all between state party identification and McGovern's vote but a moderately strong one between state ideology and McGovern's vote. In both 1976 and 1980, when Jimmy Carter, a moderate southern Democrat, was the Democratic candidate, his vote was much more strongly correlated with state party identifica-

TABLE 4.4. CORRELATIONS OF STATE PARTY IDENTIFICATION AND IDEOLOGY WITH
PRESIDENTIAL VOTE IN 1972–1984 AND 2000–2012 ELECTIONS

	Presidential election							
	1972	1976	1980	1984	2000	2004	2008	2012
State party ID	−.015	.689**	.697**	.360*	.961**	.964**	.918**	.930**
State ideology	.564**	.239	.315*	.535**	.858**	.919**	.920**	.924**

Note: Entries shown are Pearson product-moment correlation coefficients. Coefficients marked with a single asterisk are significant at the .05 level. Coefficients marked with a double asterisk are significant at the .001 level. Significance levels based on one-tailed t-tests.

Sources: For 1972–1984 elections, 1974–1982 CBS/New York Times polling data compiled by Wright, Erikson, and McIver; for 2000–2012, Gallup Poll data on 2012 state party identification. State election results from uselectionatlas.org.

tion but much more weakly correlated with state ideology. Even when Ronald Reagan, the leader of the conservative wing of the GOP, was the Republican nominee in 1980, the correlation between state ideology and the presidential vote was quite modest. In 1984, however, when another liberal northern Democrat, Walter Mondale, ran against Reagan, the correlation was stronger.

More recently, the connections between presidential election results and both state party identification and state ideology have been very different. For the four elections between 2000 and 2012, we see strong and consistent relationships between state election results and both partisanship and ideology. There is also, of course, a very strong relationship between state partisanship and state ideology. In all four of these elections, Democratic presidential candidates received their strongest support from states that were the highest in both Democratic and liberal identification while Republican presidential candidates received their strongest support from states that were the highest in both Republican and conservative identification.

TABLE 4.5. CORRELATIONS OF STATE PRESIDENTIAL ELECTION RESULTS FOR
1972–1984 AND 2000–2012

	1976	1980	1984
1972	.437***	.402**	.823***
1976		.916***	.764***
1980			.800***

	2004	2008	2012
2000	.962***	.889***	.890***
2004		.944***	.949***
2008			.983***

Note: Entries shown are Pearson product-moment correlation coefficients. Coefficients marked with a double asterisk are significant at the .01 level. Coefficients marked with a triple asterisk are significant at the .001 level. Significance levels based on one-tailed t-tests.

Source: State election results from uselectionatlas.org

The growing relationships between ideology and partisanship in the states, and between both ideology and partisanship and presidential election results in the states, have caused the outcomes of these elections to become much more consistent. This can be seen very clearly by examining the correlations among the results of presidential elections in the states during the same two electoral eras covered in the previous table. The correlations for the four elections between 1972 and 1984 are variable and sometimes weak, ranking from only .402 for the 1972–1980 elections to .916 for the 1976–1980 elections (table 4.5).

In the earlier era, the degree of consistency between election outcomes in the states depended on the parties' candidates, and especially the ideological orientation of the Democratic nominee. All of the Republican presidential candidates during this era were conservatives, although Ronald Reagan was more conservative than either Richard Nixon or Gerald Ford. In these four elections, however, there was more variability in the ideological views of the Democratic nominees.

Despite very different overall results, the 1976 and 1980 elections showed a high degree of consistency in relative levels of support because the Democratic candidate in both elections was Jimmy Carter, a relatively moderate southerner. There was very little consistency in relative levels of support between the results of the 1972 election and the results in 1976 or 1980, probably because the Democratic nominee in 1972, George McGovern, was a very liberal northerner. In fact, there was much greater consistency in relative support for the parties in the states between the 1972 and 1984 elections than between the 1972 election and either 1976 or 1980. This is almost certainly because the Democratic nominee in 1984, Walter Mondale, was also a liberal from a northern state.

In marked contrast to this pattern, the correlations among the four elections between 2000 and 2012 were consistently very strong, ranging from .89 for the 2000–2008 pair and the 2000–2012 pair to a remarkable .98 for the 2008–2012 pair. Moreover, as we have seen, forty states and the District of Columbia voted for the same party's nominee in all four elections. Even though the Democratic nominee in 2000, Al Gore of Tennessee, had been considered a moderate when he became Bill Clinton's running mate in 1992, there was little difference between the results at the state level in that election and those at the state level in 2004 and 2008, when the Democratic nominees, John Kerry and Barack Obama, were liberal northerners.

Additional evidence of the transformation of the parties' geographic bases can be seen by examining the mean swing in the Democratic share of the vote in the states and the standard deviation of the swing across all states in consecutive elections (table 4.6). We have seen that candidate choices at the individual and state levels were much more firmly anchored by both party identification and

TABLE 4.6. Size and Uniformity of Inter-Election Swings in State
Democratic Vote Share, 1972–1984 and 2000–2012

Elections	Mean swing	Standard deviation of swing
1972–1976	+ 13.4	8.6
1976–1980	– 9.0	2.9
1980–1984	– 0.6	5.3
2000–2004	– 0.1	2.0
2004–2008	+ 4.7	2.7
2008–2012	– 0.8	1.9

Note: Data are weighted by number of U.S. House districts in each state to reflect population.

Source: uselectionatlas.org

ideology in 2000–2012 than 1972–1984. As a result, inter-election vote swings were generally much smaller and more consistent across states during the later period. In 1972–1984, the average inter-election vote swing in the states was 7.7 percentage points, and the average standard deviation of the inter-election vote swing was 5.6 percentage points. But in the 2000–2012 era, the average inter-election vote swing was only 1.9 percentage points, and the average standard deviation just 2.2 percentage points.

The Great Alignment and the New Political Geography

Not only are the geographic bases of the Democratic and Republican parties very different today than they were in the 1970s and 1980s, the nation is much more polarized along geographic lines. These changes reflect the fact that since the 1970s there has been an ideological realignment of partisanship at both the individual and state levels.

Today, partisanship and ideology are very closely aligned. At the state level, this means that the most liberal state electorates are also the most Democratic while the most conservative electorates are the most Republican. Moreover, the evidence presented in this chapter shows that the changing relationship between state ideology and partisanship was the result of an ideological realignment—states that were relatively liberal in the 1970s have become increasingly Democratic, relative to the nation, while states that were relatively conservative in the 1970s have become increasingly Republican. In other words, ideology has driven partisan change; partisanship has not driven ideological change. States have remained fairly stable in their ideological orientations, even as their partisan orientations have changed remarkably. As a result, there is almost no relationship between state partisanship in the twenty-first century and state partisanship in the 1970s.

The growing alignment of state ideology and partisanship has drastically altered electoral competition in the states. Relative support for the parties at the state level is now much more consistent with both state partisanship and state ideology, in large part because partisanship and ideology now reinforce each other. Inter-election vote swings are smaller and much more consistent across states. States with relatively liberal and Democratic electorates now consistently support Democratic presidential candidates, while states with relatively conservative and Republican electorates consistently support Republican candidates.

This alignment of partisanship with ideology means that there are far fewer swing states and House districts, compared with the 1970s, and far more states and districts that strongly favor one party. In addition, the results of presidential elections are much more strongly related to the results of Senate and House elections. In elections between 1972 and 1990, the rate of partisan consistency between presidential and House outcomes was only 62 percent, and the rate of partisan consistency between presidential and Senate outcomes was only 53 percent. In the 2012–2014 elections, the rate of partisan consistency between presidential and House outcomes was 93 percent, and the rate of partisan consistency between presidential and Senate outcomes was 87 percent.

This new political geography reflects the underlying reality of a polarized electorate—an electorate in which Democratic and Republican voters themselves are sharply divided along racial, cultural, and ideological lines. In the next chapter, we will examine the characteristics and behavior of this new American electorate.

FIVE

The New American Electorate

Electoral competition in the United States has changed dramatically in recent years. Patterns of competition between the two major parties in the twenty-first century are very different from those that prevailed as recently as the 1990s. Compared with the patterns of competition that prevailed for half a century following World War II, the present era is distinguished by three main characteristics. First, at the national level, there is a close balance of support for the two major political parties, resulting in intense competition for control of Congress and the White House. Second, despite the close balance at the national level, there is widespread one-party domination of elections at the state and local level. Third, election outcomes show a very high degree of consistency over time and across different types of races. State and local elections have been increasingly nationalized: their outcomes now closely reflect the outcome of the presidential election. These characteristics are closely related. All of them reflect the central underlying reality of American electoral politics: today's electorate is strongly partisan because it is deeply divided along racial, ideological, and cultural lines.[1]

Competitive Elections

Recent national elections in the United States have been highly competitive. There have been regular shifts in party control of both chambers of Congress and the White House, and popular vote margins in presidential elections have been relatively close. Frequent changes in party control of the presidency are not a new phenomenon. Between 1948 and 1992, the White House changed hands in 1952, 1960, 1968, 1976, 1980, and 1992. However, party control of the House of Representatives and the Senate was much more stable, shifting only in 1952 and 1954 in the case of the House, and only in 1952, 1954, 1980, and 1986 in the Senate. Democrats controlled the House of Representatives for forty consecutive years between 1954 and 1994, and the Senate for thirty-four of those years. Since then, however, the House has changed hands three times—in 1994, 2006, and 2010—and the Senate has changed hands five times, in 1994, 2001 (because of a party switch by one Republican senator), 2002, 2006, and 2014.

Majorities in both chambers have generally been smaller than they were during the four decades when Democrats enjoyed almost continuous control of the legislative branch. During the heyday of Democratic domination, between the 84th Congress (1955–1957) and the 103rd (1993–1995), the average Senate majority was 58 seats and the average House majority was 261 seats. In contrast, between the 104th Congress (1995–1997) and the 113th Congress (2013–2015), the average Senate majority was only 54 seats and the average House majority only 232 seats. These smaller majorities meant that party control of both chambers was at stake in almost every election.

While changes in party control of the White House occurred frequently between the 1950s and 1990s, many elections during those years were decided by very large popular vote margins. The popular vote margins in recent presidential elections have been narrower. Of course, there have been closely contested presidential elections throughout American history, but there have also been many landslides in which one candidate defeated his opponent by ten percentage points or more in the popular vote. During most of the twentieth century, landslide elections were the rule and not the exception. Ten of the seventeen presidential elections between 1920 and 1984 were won by a double-digit margin. However, since Ronald Reagan's 18-point drubbing of Walter Mondale in 1984, there has not been a landslide presidential election. The average popular vote margin in presidential elections fell from 13.9 percentage points between 1920 and 1984 to only 5.1 percentage points between 1988 and 2012. Not since the late nineteenth century has the United States had such a long series of closely contested presidential elections.

Recent presidential elections have not only been considerably closer on average than earlier ones but also more stable. Through most of the twentieth century, it was not unusual for the popular vote margin between the Democratic and Republican candidates to fluctuate widely from one election to the next. Between 1928 and 1932, for example, the Republican share of the national popular vote fell from over 58 percent to less than 40 percent. The five elections between 1956 and 1972 included Republican landslides in '56 and '72, a Democratic landslide in '64, and closely contested elections in '60 and '68. The party vote shares in recent presidential contests have varied a good deal less.

In order to examine trends in competition in the sixteen presidential elections between 1952 and 2012, I divided them into four eras of four elections each: 1952–1964, 1968–1980, 1984–1996, and

TABLE 5.1. COMPETITION IN U.S. PRESIDENTIAL ELECTIONS SINCE 1952

Elections	Average winning margin	Standard deviation
1952–1964	12.5	17.3
1968–1980	9.0	11.9
1984–1996	9.8	12.1
2000–2012	3.5	4.4

Note: Entries shown are percentages.

Source: uselectionsatlas.org

2000–2012. For each era, I calculated the average popular vote margin of the winning candidate and the standard deviation of the margin of victory or defeat of the Democratic candidate (table 5.1). The data show a striking pattern. The elections during the first era, between 1952 and 1964, show both the largest average margin of victory and the largest standard deviation. Average margins of victory and standard deviations were somewhat smaller in the second and third eras, but the most dramatic change occurs in the most recent era. The four presidential elections between 2000 and 2012 have had by far the closest average margins of victory and by far the smallest variability from election to election of any of the four eras. In fact, the four most recent presidential elections had the closest popular vote margins and the least election-to-election variability of any set of four consecutive presidential elections in the past century. To find a series of presidential elections with outcomes as close and as stable as these, you have to go back to the last quarter of the nineteenth century.

One-Party Dominance of State and Local Elections

Despite the competitiveness of presidential and congressional elections, there has been a marked decline in the competitiveness of elections at the state and local levels. There are far fewer swing states and congressional districts, and far more strongly Democratic and Republican states and districts now than in the 1960s and '70s. What is striking about the presidential election of 2012 is that despite the closeness of the national popular vote, there were very few closely contested states. Only four states were decided by a margin of less than 5 percentage points—Florida, Ohio, Virginia, and North Carolina. Twenty-seven states, as well as the District of Columbia, were decided by at least 15 percentage points. Mitt Romney actually carried more states by landslide and near-landslide margins than Barack Obama, but the states Obama carried had far more electoral votes.

The 2012 results continued the recent pattern of presidential elections that are decided by narrow margins at the national level but by landslide or near-landslide margins in many states, including some of the most populous and electoral-vote-rich states in the country. Thus, President Obama carried California with its 55 electoral votes by 23 points, New York (29 electoral votes) by 28 points, and Illinois (20 electoral votes) by 17. Mitt Romney won Texas's 38 electoral votes by a margin of 16 points.

This pattern of many deep red and blue states, including several of the nation's most populous, represents a dramatic change from the pattern seen in close presidential elections during the 1960s and 1970s. In 1960 and 1976, when John F. Kennedy and Jimmy Carter won close, hard-fought battles for the White House, twenty states were decided by a margin of less than 5 percentage points. Moreover, in those elections almost all of the nation's most populous states were closely contested. In 1976, states decided by less than 5 points accounted for 299 electoral votes, while states decided by 15 points or more accounted for only 66 electoral votes. In 2012, in contrast, states decided by less than 5 points accounted for only 75 electoral votes while states decided by 15 points or more accounted for 289.

Because there are so many deep red and blue states, it is easy to predict which party's candidate will carry the large majority of states long before Election Day. Long before the Republican candidate in 2012 was known, there was very little doubt about how at least thirty-five states would cast their electoral votes. In the end, forty-eight of the fifty states along with the District of Columbia supported the same party in 2012 as in 2008. Only Indiana and North Carolina switched sides—both from the Democratic column to the Republican—between the two elections.

The decline in the number of competitive states has been paralleled by a similar trend at the congressional district level. Far more House districts today are dominated by one party and far fewer are closely divided. We can compare, for instance, presidential election results at the House district level in 1976 and 2012. Although the national margins of victory were similar, the results at the congressional district level were very different. In 1976, out of 435 House districts, one of the presidential candidates won by at least 20 percentage points in only 26 districts, while 187 districts were won by a margin of less than 5 percentage points. In 2012, a majority of House districts, 232 out of 435, were won by a margin of at least 20 percentage points in the presidential election, and only 47 were won by a margin of less than 5 percentage points. This change means that in the current Congress, unlike earlier Congresses, the majority of House members from both parties represent safe districts. These representatives have little need to be concerned about the views of voters from the opposing party. Instead, they worry about their own party's primary voters, because the dominant party's primary is the only election that matters in these districts—the winner is almost certain to win the general election.

Some political observers have attributed the recent decline in competitive districts to partisan gerrymandering. But a comparison of the partisan composition of House districts before and after redistricting in 1980–1982, 1990–1992, and 2000–2002 did not reveal significant differences in the districts' competitiveness. Most of the decline in competitiveness actually occurred between redistricting cycles.[2] An examination of redistricting at the state legislative level as well found that partisan gerrymandering had little impact on either competition or polarization.[3] Moreover, as we have seen, competitiveness has also declined in statewide elections, even though state boundaries are fixed, and in county elections. The proportion of Americans living in "landslide counties," those that one party's presidential candidate carried by at least 20 percentage points, has been growing, while the proportion living in highly competitive counties has been shrinking.[4] These trends clearly cannot be explained by clever line-drawing to protect incumbents. We have to look to deeper trends in American society.

Consistency of Election Results

The third major feature of recent electoral competition in the United States is a very high degree of consistency in voters' preferences, and therefore in the outcomes of elections at the state and local levels as well as at the national level. Not only have the election-to-election swings in the national popular vote been much smaller than in earlier decades, they have also been exceptionally stable. Only two states, Indiana and North Carolina, switched sides between the 2008 and 2012 presidential elections—the smallest number of states to do so in consecutive presidential elections since the end of World War II. Moreover, the correlation between the Democratic share of the vote in 2008 and the Democratic share of the vote in 2012 across all fifty states and the District of Columbia was a remarkable .98. This was the strongest correlation between two consecutive elections in the postwar era. The Democratic share of the vote in 2008 almost perfectly predicted the Democratic share of the vote in 2012. And the correlation between the Democratic share of the vote in 2004 and the Democratic share of the vote in 2012, two elections eight years apart with totally different sets of candidates, was almost as large at .95. The correlations were just as strong at the congressional district and county levels.

Recent elections have also been marked by an extraordinary degree of consistency in electoral outcomes at different levels.[5] The correlation between the Democratic share of the presidential vote and the Democratic share of the vote for U.S. House of Representatives across all districts with contested House races in 2012 was .95. This was the highest correlation between presidential and U.S. House election results in the post–World War II era. Only 25 out of 435 House districts were won by a candidate from the opposite party from the presidential candidate who carried that district. In the 113th Congress, only 16 Republicans represented districts carried by Barack Obama, and only 9 Democrats represented districts carried by Mitt Romney. And this pattern continued to hold in the 115th Congress, which was elected in 2016. In 2017, only 23 Republicans represented districts carried by Hillary Clinton, while only 12 Democrats represented districts carried by Donald Trump.

Although results of Senate elections have not been quite so consistent with presidential voting, there has been a marked increase in the relationship between presidential and Senate election outcomes. The vast majority of U.S. senators now come from the same party as the winner of the most recent presidential election in their state. The 26 states carried by Barack Obama in 2012 were represented by 43 Democrats and 9 Republicans in the 113th Congress, while the 24 states carried by Mitt Romney were represented by 12 Democrats and 36 Republicans.

As in the case of the House, this pattern continued to hold in the 115th Congress, which was elected in 2016. In 2017, the 20 states carried by Hillary Clinton in 2016 were represented by 37 Democrats and 3 Republicans, while the 30 states carried by Donald Trump were represented by 11 Democrats and 49 Republicans. There has also been a decline in the number of states with split-party Senate delegations over the past forty years. In the 93rd Congress (1973–1975), 24 states had split-party delegations. In the 115th Congress (2017–2019), only 12 states had split-party delegations. Most were swing states like Ohio, Florida, Wisconsin, and Pennsylvania.

The growing consistency of election results extends all the way down to state legislative races. The party composition of state legislatures is now strongly related to the results of presidential elections. The correlation between the Democratic share of the presidential vote in 2012 and the Democratic share of state legislative seats in 2012 was .85, the strongest correlation between presidential and state legislative election results for any year since at least 1956. Since the midterm election of 2010, Republicans have controlled most of the nation's state legislative chambers. Nevertheless, in the 26 states carried by Barack Obama in 2012, Democrats controlled 37 out of 52 legislative chambers following that year's elections. In the 23 states with partisan legislatures (Nebraska has a nonpartisan unicameral legislature) carried by Mitt Romney, Republicans controlled 43 out of 46 legislative chambers following the 2012 elections. Altogether, over 80 percent of partisan state legislative chambers in 2013 were controlled by the party whose presidential candidate carried the state in 2012. And this pattern was even stronger in 2017, with 89 of 98 chambers, or 91 percent, controlled by the party whose presidential candidate carried the state in 2016.

The remarkable consistency in the results of recent presidential elections, and between the results of presidential, congressional, and state legislative elections, can be explained by the sharp division in today's American electorate. All of these election results closely reflected the underlying strength of the parties in the states and districts and the fact that, although the nation as a whole is closely divided, the large majority of states and congressional districts now clearly favor one party or the other. As a result, the outcomes of presidential elections and control of the House and Senate are determined by the few swing states and districts where the outcome is in doubt—a group whose number has been steadily decreasing.

In 2012, the partisan divide was clearly evident at the individual level as well. According to the national exit poll, 93 percent of Republican identifiers voted for Romney while 92 percent of Democratic identifiers voted for Obama. This was the highest level of party loyalty in any presidential election since the beginning of exit polls in 1972, and it continued a pattern of strong partisan voting in recent presidential elections. Data from the 2012 American National Election Study confirm this pattern: 91 percent of party identifiers, including leaning independents, voted for their own party's presidential candidate, while only 7 percent defected to the opposing party's candidate. This was the highest level of party loyalty in any presidential election since the ANES began asking about party identification in 1952.

Data from the 2012 survey also show a very high degree of stability in presidential voting between 2008 and 2012. Among those who reported voting in both elections, 92 percent supported the same party both times. Over 93 percent of McCain supporters in 2008 voted for Mitt Romney in 2012, while over 90 percent of Obama supporters in 2008 voted for him again in 2012. Ninety-eight percent of strong Democrats, 81 percent of weak Democrats, and 85 percent of independent Democrats reported voting for Obama in both elections. Likewise, 95 percent of strong Republicans, 81 percent of weak Republicans, and 81 percent of independent Republicans said they voted for McCain in 2008 and Romney in 2012.

The 92 percent who voted for the same party in 2008 and 2012 was the highest for any pair of consecutive elections for which data are available. Although the ANES has not generally asked respondents about their presidential vote in the previous election, national exit polls have included such a question for some time. These data suggest that the proportion of swing voters has been declining since the 1970s.

The record for stability of party voting in elections without a significant third party or independent candidate was set in 2000–2004, two elections in which George W. Bush was on the ballot. According to the 2004 national exit poll, 91 percent of those voting in both elections cast their ballots for the same party—90 percent of 2000 Gore voters chose John Kerry in 2004 and 91 percent of 2000 Bush voters chose Bush again in 2004. Partisan consistency was slightly lower between 2004 and 2008—at 86 percent—and between 1984 and 1988, when it was 85 percent. However, it was only 76 percent between 1972 and 1976. Almost one in four voters switched parties between those two elections, and the switches went in both directions—26 percent of those voting for Richard Nixon in 1972 switched to Jimmy Carter in 1976, and 18 percent of those voting for George McGovern in 1972 switched to Gerald Ford in 1976. This high rate of instability between consecutive elections suggests that even though the proportion of voters identifying with a party hardly changed from the 1970s to the 2000s, the influence of partisanship was much weaker.

Party loyalty is by no means confined to presidential voting. According to the 2012 national exit poll, 94 percent of Democrats voted for the Democratic candidate for the House of Representatives and 94 percent of Republicans voted for the Republican candidate. Ticket splitting was rare. According to the 2012 national exit poll, 91 percent of voters cast a straight-party vote in the presidential and U.S. House elections. Again, results from the 2012 ANES were similar: 89 percent of Democrats and 93 percent of Republicans voted for their party's House candidate, and 90 percent of all voters cast a straight-party ballot in the presidential and House elections.

How Polarized Is the American Electorate?

The results of recent elections at all levels of American government show that the U.S. electorate is sharply divided along racial, cultural, and ideological lines. These divisions explain the record levels of party loyalty and straight-ticket voting in these contests. But does this mean that the parties in the electorate are also polarized? Could these trends just reflect, as some scholars have argued, that the two major parties' supporters are better sorted along ideological lines?

According to Morris Fiorina and others, Americans today are better sorted by party than they were thirty or forty years ago, but they are no more polarized. By this, Fiorina means that party identification today is more closely related to ideology, values, and specific issue positions than it was in the past. Democrats and Republicans are more likely to be found on the opposite sides of these divides, but the distribution of opinion is still a bell-shaped curve, with most of us near the center where we have always been. The large majority of Americans, according to Fiorina, hold moderate views. It is the elites and activists who are divided into polarized camps with few centrists, not the voters.[6]

It is certainly possible for voters to become increasingly sorted but not increasingly polarized. But the evidence from the ANES does not support this conclusion. Instead it shows that in practice, sorting and polarization are almost indistinguishable. As the American electorate has become increasingly sorted by party, the distributions of ideological positions, policy preferences, and even candidate evaluations have become increasingly polarized, with fewer Democrats and Republicans found near the center and more near the opposing attitudinal poles. But this shift toward the extremes has not always affected supporters of both parties equally. On some questions, Republicans have moved further to the right than Democrats have moved to the left.

Asymmetrical Polarization:
The Case of Ideological Identification

Between 1972, the first time the ANES survey included a question on ideology, and 2012, there was a gradual but ultimately quite dramatic change in the relative positions of Democratic and Republican voters on the seven-point ideology scale, where 1 represents the extreme left, 7 the extreme right, and 4 the exact center. The average Democratic voter moved from a mean location of 3.8, or just left of center, to 3.4. Over the same period, the average Republican voter moved from a mean location of 4.6 to 5.3. As a result of these shifts, the distance between the average Democratic voter and the average Republican voter more than doubled, going from 0.8 units in 1972 to 2.0 units in 2012, but 64 percent of this increase was due to the rightward movement of Republican voters.

The significance of these changes can be seen by directly comparing the distributions of Democratic and Republican voters on the ideology scale in these two years (table 5.2). Between 1972 and 2012, the proportion of Democratic voters placing themselves in the center of the scale (or unable to place themselves) fell from 52 percent to 41 percent, while the proportion placing themselves on the left side of the scale increased from 29 percent to 47 percent. The change among Republican voters was considerably greater. Between 1972 and 2012, the proportion of Republican voters placing themselves in the center or unable to place themselves fell from 44 percent to 22 percent, while the proportion placing themselves on the right side of the scale increased from 46 percent to 75 percent.

As the two parties' supporters were moving apart over these forty years, the shape of the distribution was also changing. The propor-

TABLE 5.2. DISTRIBUTIONS OF DEMOCRATIC AND REPUBLICAN VOTERS ON
IDEOLOGY SCALE IN 1972 AND 2012

Ideology	Democratic voters		Republican voters	
	1972	2012	1972	2012
Very liberal	16	28	2	1
Lean liberal	13	19	8	2
Moderate, none	52	41	44	22
Lean conservative	11	11	25	25
Very conservative	7	1	21	51

Note: Very liberal = 1, 2; Lean liberal = 3; Moderate, none, or haven't thought about it = 4; Lean conservative = 5; Very conservative = 6, 7. Entries shown are percentages.

Source: American National Election Studies

tion of all voters placing themselves in the center of the scale or unable to place themselves fell from 49 percent in 1972 to 35 percent in 2012. At the same time, the proportion placing themselves at or close to the left or right poles of the scale—at 1, 2, 6, or 7—increased from 23 percent in 1972 to 39 percent in 2012. In 1972, more than twice as many voters placed themselves in the center or could not place themselves than called themselves strong ideologues. By 2012, strong ideologues outnumbered those in the center or unable to place themselves.

The changing distribution of voters on the ideology scale can also be seen when we compare the standard deviation of the scale in 1972 with that of 2012. The standard deviation of the scale is a direct measure of the intensity of disagreement within the electorate over ideology: the larger it is, the more intense the disagreement. Like the distance between the parties, the standard deviation of the ideology scale grew gradually but steadily over these forty years. In 1972, it was 1.15 units for all voters. By 2012, it had increased to 1.46 units, an increase of 27 percent.

The changes in the locations of Democratic and Republican

voters and the change in the overall distribution of voters on the seven-point ideology scale show that party sorting and polarization have occurred simultaneously. Since the early 1970s, Democrats have shifted to the left, Republicans have shifted even further to the right, and the overall distribution has shifted away from the center and toward the two ends. These shifts are very similar to those seen among members of the U.S. Senate and House of Representatives during the same period, although the shifts in Congress have been somewhat larger. Nevertheless, the evidence shows very clearly that for both groups, sorting and polarization are very closely connected. As Democrats and Republicans in the electorate and in Congress have sorted themselves across the ideological divide, they have simultaneously moved away from the center.

Constraint and Polarization on Social Welfare Issues

The significance of increased sorting and polarization depends on how strongly voters' positions on the ANES scale correlate with their positions on specific policy issues. Some early research on ideological identification suggested that this scale measured largely symbolic attitudes and was only weakly related to actual policy preferences.[7] Today, however, ideological identification is strongly related to positions on a wide range of issues, especially social welfare issues. Moreover, opinions on these issues have themselves become much more closely connected over time. In other words, to use the term coined by Philip Converse in "The Nature of Belief Systems in Mass Publics," his classic study of ideological thinking, voters' opinions on these issues have become more constrained.[8]

According to Converse, issue constraint is a key characteristic of ideological thinking: to the extent that opinions on different issues are shaped by an underlying worldview or ideology, they should be related. He found that constraint was very weak in the American mass public in the 1950s and concluded that ideology was largely confined to political elites and activists. The question for us is whether this has changed since Converse conducted his pioneering research.

Unfortunately, we do not have public opinion data on issue questions that have been asked consistently since the 1950s. In fact, the questions Converse used to measure issue constraint in the electorate were considered so flawed that they were abandoned shortly after his study was published. However, we do have data on a series of four social welfare policy issues, which, along with the ideology question, have been asked consistently in every presidential election survey since 1984. These issue questions, like the ideology question, ask respondents to place themselves on seven-point scales. They ask about government aid to improve the condition of black Americans, government versus individual responsibility for jobs and living standards, reliance on government versus private companies for health insurance, and the trade-off between government services and spending and taxes. As with the ideology question, I have assigned respondents who declined to place themselves on each of these questions to the middle position.

An analysis of the responses to these four questions shows that even over the fairly short span of twenty-eight years, issue constraint increased substantially. The average correlation among the four social welfare questions increased from .29 in 1984 to .50 in 2012, while the average correlation between the social welfare issue questions and the ideology question increasing from .25 in 1984 to .47 in 2012. In terms of shared variance, the relationships among opinions on these questions were about three times stronger in 2012 than in 1984.

These findings indicate that ideological thinking was much more prevalent in the American electorate in 2012 than in 1984. Moreover, issue constraint is an important indicator of ideological polarization. Higher levels of constraint mean that a larger proportion of

TABLE 5.3. DISTRIBUTIONS OF DEMOCRATIC AND REPUBLICAN VOTERS ON
SOCIAL WELFARE ATTITUDES SCALE IN 1984 AND 2012

Social welfare scale score	Democratic voters		Republican voters	
	1972	2012	1972	2012
Very liberal	8	8	1	0
Lean liberal	26	32	8	2
Moderate	52	45	43	17
Lean conservative	13	14	39	42
Very conservative	1	1	9	38

Note: Entries shown are percentages.

Source: American National Election Studies

voters hold consistently liberal or consistently conservative opinions, and a smaller proportion have a mixture of liberal and conservative opinions. The magnitude of the increase in ideological polarization can be seen by comparing the distributions of Democratic and Republican voters on a social welfare issues scale based on responses to the four questions described above (table 5.3).

The results show that, like ideology, opinions on social welfare issues have become asymmetrically polarized. Between 1984 and 2012, the proportion of voters in the center of the social welfare issues scale fell from 48 percent to 32 percent, while the proportion located close to the poles rose from 10 percent to 23 percent. Almost all of the increase, however, was due to the growing conservatism of Republican voters. Democratic voters shifted only slightly to the left between 1984 and 2012—the proportion of moderates fell from 52 percent to 45 percent while the proportion of liberals rose from 33 percent to 40 percent. And the proportion of strong liberals among Democratic voters did not increase at all. They made up only 8 percent of Democratic voters in both 2012 and 1984. Republicans, meanwhile, shifted dramatically to the right on social welfare issues during these years. The proportion of moderates and liberals combined fell from 52 percent to 20 percent, while the proportion of conservatives rose from 48 percent to 80 percent, and of strong conservatives from 9 percent to 38 percent.

Symmetrical Polarization: Cultural Issues

A similar pattern of asymmetrical polarization is found in Congress. Since the 1970s, analyses of roll-call votes have shown that Republicans in both the Senate and the House have moved much further to the right than Democrats in either chamber have moved to the left. In both Congress and the electorate, conservatives now greatly outnumber moderates and liberals among Republicans. Liberals do not greatly outnumber moderates and conservatives among Democrats. However, this pattern does not hold for all issues. When it comes to cultural issues such as abortion and gay rights, Democratic voters now appear to be at least as far to the left as Republican voters are to the right.

To measure opinions on cultural issues, I created a scale combining two questions on abortion policy and two questions on gay rights in the 2012 ANES. The abortion questions were the traditional four-point ANES abortion policy scale and a nine-point scale measuring support or opposition to abortion as a woman's choice. The gay rights questions asked about same-sex marriage and adoption rights. Opinions on these questions were rather closely connected, with correlations ranging from .42 to .71 and an average correlation of .53.

When we compare the distributions of Democratic and Republican voters on the five-point cultural issues scale, it is clear that opinions were quite polarized in 2012 (figure 5.1). Over half of all voters were classified as either strong liberals (34 percent) or strong conservatives (22 percent). Only 12 percent were classified as moderates. There was also a sharp divide between the parties. However, on cultural issues, unlike social welfare issues, Democratic voters

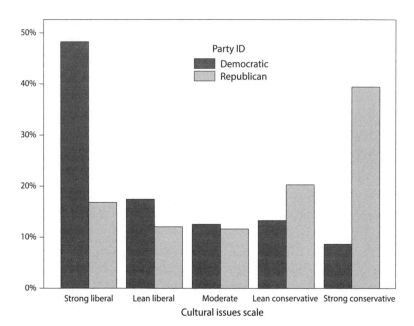

Figure 5.1. Distributions of Democratic and Republican Voters on Cultural Issues Scale in 2012. Source: 2012 American National Election Study

were somewhat further to the left of center than Republican voters were to the right of center. Sixty-six percent of Democratic voters were classified as liberals and 48 percent as strong liberals on cultural issues, while 60 percent of Republican voters were classified as conservatives and 40 percent as strong conservatives.

Despite these different patterns of polarization on social welfare and cultural issues, we see sharp differences between the two major parties on both types of issues. Moreover, there is a growing connection between these two types of issues. Voters in the liberal or conservative camp on social welfare issues are increasingly in the same camp on cultural issues. We can see this when we examine the correlation between location on the social welfare issues scale and opinion on the four-point abortion policy scale since 1984—the abortion scale being the one cultural issue that has been included in ANES surveys over that time. The relationship between opinions on these two types of issues has grown steadily stronger, with the correlation coefficients increasing from .01 in 1984 to .04 in 1988, .11 in 1992, .13 in 1996 and 2000, .18 in 2004, .23 in 2008, and .28 in 2012. In addition, the correlation between the cultural issues scale and the social welfare issues scale in 2012 was an even stronger .36. It is clear that opinions on these types of issues are increasingly likely to reinforce one another, and thus to push voters in the same partisan direction. Moreover, there was even greater consistency between cultural and social welfare policy preferences among more politically active voters. The correlation between cultural conservatism and social welfare conservatism was .49 among ANES respondents who reported engaging in three or more campaign activities beyond voting, compared with .30 among those who engaged in no activities beyond voting.

Affective Polarization

The rise of partisan polarization over the past four decades has involved voters' feelings about the parties and candidates as well as their ideological and issue positions. Because of the rise of negative partisanship, affective polarization has grown even more than issue or ideological polarization. This can be seen by examining the trends in relative feeling thermometer evaluations of the Democratic and Republican presidential candidates between 1968, the first time the feeling thermometer was included in the ANES survey, and 2012 (table 5.4). The statistics shown in this table are the average difference between the feeling thermometer ratings of the candidates by Democratic and Republican voters and the standard deviation of the feeling thermometer difference scores for all voters. The former

TABLE 5.4. THE RISE OF AFFECTIVE POLARIZATION: FEELING THERMOMETER
RATINGS OF PRESIDENTIAL CANDIDATES, 1972–2012

Year	Party difference	Standard deviation
1968	46.8	38.6
1972	54.5	47.9
1976	47.9	40.1
1980	55.5	43.7
1984	71.8	49.0
1988	67.6	46.6
1992	63.6	44.3
1996	69.0	47.1
2000	63.8	44.0
2004	91.4	56.7
2008	72.3	48.9
2012	105.2	62.3

Source: American National Election Studies

statistic measures the size of the divide between the parties, while
the latter measures the overall divide in evaluations of the candidates within the electorate.

Both the average difference between the relative thermometer
ratings of Democrats and Republicans and the overall dispersion of
these ratings have increased substantially over this period, and especially since 2000. The 2012 election set new records for both
measures. Moreover, the increase in affective polarization in recent years has been fairly symmetrical. Both Democrats and Republicans now favor their own party's presidential candidate over
the opposing party's candidate much more strongly than in the past,
especially in elections involving an incumbent. Both the Bush-Kerry
contest in 2004 and the Obama-Romney contest in 2012 produced
very strong preferences by partisans for their party's standard-
bearer. In 2004, Republicans rated George W. Bush an average of
50 degrees higher than John Kerry, while Democrats rated Kerry an

average of 41 degrees higher than Bush. In 2012, Democrats rated Barack Obama an average of 55 degrees higher than Mitt Romney, while Republicans rated Romney an average of 50 degrees higher than Obama.

Contrary to claims by some scholars that affective polarization is distinct from ideological and issue polarization,[9] the recent increase in affective polarization is closely connected with the increase in polarization over issues and ideology. Democratic and Republican voters prefer their party's candidates more intensely than in the past because they prefer their party's ideology and policy positions more intensely. Thus, the correlation between ideology and relative feeling thermometer ratings increased from .47 in 1984 to .66 in 2012. Over the same period, the correlation between location on the social welfare issues scale and relative feeling thermometer ratings increased from .53 to .72.

The large increase in partisan polarization on relative thermometer ratings of the presidential candidates between 1984 and 2012 is especially impressive given that the choices presented to the voters appeared to be no more polarized in 2012 than in 1984. It would be difficult to find evidence that Barack Obama was a more liberal Democrat than Walter Mondale, who had a consistently liberal voting record during his years in the U.S. Senate, or that Mitt Romney was a more conservative Republican than Ronald Reagan, who was widely seen as the leading conservative within the Republican Party before his election as president in 1980.

These results contradict the claim by Fiorina and his co-authors that today's more divided voter evaluations of political leaders reflect more polarized choices, not more polarized voter positions.[10] In fact, the difference in affective polarization between 1984 and 2012 can only be explained by a growing divide between Democratic and Republican voters on ideology and policy. Presenting polarized candidate choices to an overwhelmingly centrist electorate should yield mainly indifferent evaluations from voters. Only voters who are ideologically on one side or the other would be expected to have strong preferences between two candidates on opposite sides of that divide. The polarized evaluations of candidates seen in 2012 require both polarized candidate choices and polarized voter positions on issues and ideology.

Attitudinal Consistency, Ideological Polarization, and Partisanship

There is a very close connection between the past few decades' rise in ideological polarization and increasing partisan intensity and loyalty. It is precisely the voters with the strongest ideological convictions and the most consistent opinions across policy issues who are the strongest and most loyal partisans. According to data from the 2012 ANES, 60 percent of strong liberals, those who placed themselves at 1 or 2 on the seven-point ideology scale, identified themselves as strong Democrats, compared with only 38 percent of liberals who placed themselves at 3 on the scale. Similarly, 50 percent of strong conservatives, those who placed themselves at 6 or 7 on the ideology scale, identified themselves as strong Republicans, compared with only 11 percent of moderate conservatives who placed themselves at 5 on the scale. The results were very similar with regard to the five-item government activism scale. Sixty percent of very consistent liberals identified themselves as strong Democrats compared with only 38 percent of less consistent liberals. Likewise, 45 percent of very consistent conservatives identified themselves as strong Republicans compared with only 21 percent of less consistent conservatives.

Strength of ideological identification and issue consistency were also strongly related to party loyalty and straight-ticket voting. Ninety-nine percent of strongly liberal Democrats voted for Barack Obama for president, and 95 percent voted a straight Democratic ticket for president, U.S. House, and U.S. Senate. However, only 88 percent of moderate-to-conservative Democrats voted for Obama for president, and only 75 percent voted a straight Democratic ticket for president, House, and Senate. Ninety-eight percent of strongly conservative Republicans voted for Mitt Romney for president and 92 percent voted a straight Republican ticket for president, House, and Senate, while only 83 percent of moderate-to-liberal Republicans voted for Romney and only 63 percent voted a straight Republican ticket.

Again, results were similar with regard to the five-item government activism scale. Ninety-eight percent of consistently liberal Democratic identifiers voted for Barack Obama for president and 97 percent voted a straight Democratic ticket for president, House, and Senate. However, only 72 percent of conservative Democrats voted for Obama and only 63 percent voted a straight Democratic ticket. On the Republican side, 99 percent of consistently conservative Republican identifiers voted for Mitt Romney for president and 93 percent voted a straight Republican ticket, while only 78 percent of moderate-to-liberal Republicans voted for Romney and only 63 percent voted a straight Republican ticket. There is now a very close connection between ideological polarization and partisanship. Growing ideological polarization has been a key factor in the growth of partisan intensity over the past thirty years.

Consistency on Social Welfare and Cultural Issues

Another way to examine the consequences of attitudinal consistency is by comparing voters' positions on the five-item role-of-government scale with their positions on the four-item cultural issues scale. The cultural issues scale is based on responses to two questions on abortion policy and two questions on gay rights. There was a fairly strong relationship between voters' opinions on the role and size of government and their opinions on cultural issues—

TABLE 5.5. OPINIONS OF VOTERS ON ROLE OF GOVERNMENT
AND CULTURAL ISSUES SCALES

Cultural issues scale	Role of government scale		
	Liberal	Moderate	Conservative
Liberal	19	13	8
Moderate	8	9	7
Conservative	6	10	20

Note: Entries shown are percentages in combined categories.

Source: 2012 American National Election Study

the correlation between these two scales was .36. Based on their locations on these two scales, I divided voters into five approximately equal-sized categories: consistent liberals, moderate liberals (liberal on one scale and moderate on the other), moderates or inconsistents (moderate on both scales or liberal on one and conservative on the other), moderate conservatives (conservative on one scale and moderate on the other), and consistent conservatives (table 5.5).

The largest proportion of voters in 2012 were consistent liberals or consistent conservatives. These two groups were about equal in size, and together they made up 39 percent of the electorate. Another 38 percent of voters were liberal or conservative on one scale and moderate on the other—21 percent were moderate liberals and 17 percent moderate conservatives. The remaining 23 percent of voters were either moderate on both scales (9 percent) or inconsistent, favoring the liberal side on one set of issues and the conservative side on the other (14 percent). Eight percent of voters were classified as "libertarians," conservative on the size and role of government and liberal on cultural issues, while 6 percent were "populists," liberal on the size and role of government and conservative on cultural issues.

One thing that is immediately apparent from these findings is that those who took consistent positions on the role of government and cultural issues scales far outnumbered those who took inconsistent positions. Moreover, the percentage of respondents with consistent views was considerably greater among the highly educated than among the less educated, and considerably greater among the politically active than among the politically inactive. Consistent liberals and conservatives made up 46 percent of respondents with a post-college education but just 31 percent of those with only a high school education. Similarly, consistent liberals and conservatives made up 46 percent of politically active respondents, who engaged in two or more activities beyond voting, compared with 24 percent of politically inactive respondents.

Voters' positions on these two scales had a powerful influence on their partisan orientations and voting decisions. Consistent liberals and conservatives were far more likely than other voters to identify strongly with a party, and far more likely to vote for that party's candidates. This influence can be seen by examining respondents' presidential votes in relation to their positions on the two scales (table 5.6). Ideologically consistent voters were extremely loyal partisans: 96 percent of consistent liberals reported voting for Barack Obama for president, while 96 percent of consistent conservatives reported voting for Mitt Romney. Moderate liberals and conservatives were not quite as loyal—about 80 percent of moderately liberal respondents voted for Obama and about 80 percent of moderately conservative respondents voted for Romney. But respondents' positions on the role-of-government scale clearly had a stronger influence than their positions on the cultural-issues scale. This becomes clear when we examine the voting decisions of the most inconsistent respondents—those with liberal positions on one scale and conservative positions on the other. Libertarians voted almost three-to-one for Mitt Romney over Barack Obama, but populists voted almost three-to-one for Obama over Romney.

TABLE 5.6. PERCENTAGE VOTING FOR OBAMA BY POSITIONS ON ROLE OF
GOVERNMENT AND CULTURAL ISSUES SCALES

Cultural issues scale	Role of government scale		
	Liberal	Moderate	Conservative
Liberal	96	75	26
Moderate	91	60	9
Conservative	73	32	4

Source: 2012 American National Election Study

Consistency of voters' opinions on social welfare and cultural issues was also strongly related to stability of presidential voting between 2008 and 2012. Ninety-five percent of consistent liberals reported voting for Barack Obama in both elections, while 92 percent of consistent conservatives reported voting for John McCain in 2008 and Mitt Romney in 2012. Those with inconsistent views were much more likely to be swing voters. Fifteen percent of populists and 17 percent of libertarians reported switching parties between 2008 and 2012.

The latter groups also had distinctive social characteristics. The most striking difference between libertarians and consistent conservatives involved their religious beliefs and behavior. Libertarians were much less religious than consistent conservatives: only 21 percent reported attending religious services at least once or twice a month, compared with 67 percent of consistent conservatives. In other respects, however, the two groups were similar. Contrary to most popular descriptions, libertarians were not disproportionately young voters. Only 11 percent were eighteen to twenty-nine years of age, similar to the 14 percent of consistent conservatives who were under thirty. In contrast, eighteen to twenty-nine-year-olds made up 20 percent of consistent liberals. Sixty-eight percent of libertarians identified with or leaned toward the Republican Party.

Populists differed in several ways from consistent liberals. Compared with consistent liberals, populists were much less likely to be white, much less educated, and much more religious. Nonwhites made up 55 percent of voters with populist views, compared with only 29 percent of voters with consistently liberal views. And only 18 percent of populists were college graduates, compared with 48 percent of consistent liberals. Finally, 68 percent of populists reported attending religious services at least once or twice a month, compared with only 24 percent of consistent liberals. Despite these differences, however, 67 percent of populists identified with or leaned toward the Democratic Party.

All Politics Is National

There is no "disconnect" between political elites and the American public: America is a polarized country whose leaders reflect the diverging priorities and values of the constituents who elected them.[11] Today's Democratic electoral base is dominated by nonwhites and secular white liberals who view Republican politicians and voters alike as religious zealots, racial bigots, and defenders of multinational corporations and the wealthy. The Democratic base is pro-government, pro-choice on abortion, and pro-gay-marriage. Today's Republican electoral base is dominated by socially and economically conservative white voters who viewed Barack Obama as an extreme liberal or socialist and his supporters as unpatriotic moochers who would rather live off of government handouts than work for a living. The Republican base is anti-government, anti-choice on abortion, and opposed to gay marriage.

Voters' opinions on social welfare and cultural issues have become increasingly aligned. Voters with consistently liberal or consistently conservative views on social welfare and cultural issues now greatly outnumber those with inconsistent views. Nevertheless, each party's electoral base includes a minority of identifiers who hold views on social issues that run contrary to the dominant position within the party. Libertarians, those with relatively conservative views on social welfare issues but relatively liberal views on cultural issues, make up about 8 percent of the overall electorate and about 13 percent of Republican voters. Populists, those with liberal views on social welfare issues but conservative views on cultural issues, make up about 6 percent of the overall electorate and about 10 percent of Democratic voters.

Of the latter two groups, libertarians appear to represent a greater threat to party unity. Not only do they comprise a somewhat larger share of Republican voters than populists do of Democratic voters, they are also more politically engaged. Libertarians made up 17 percent of active Republican voters, those who engaged in two or more activities beyond voting, in 2012 whereas populists made up only 8 percent of active Democratic voters. Nevertheless, libertarians were greatly outnumbered within the Republican Party by consistent conservatives.

Because the two party bases are roughly equal in size and loyalty, elections tend to be highly competitive at the national level, which further fuels partisan conflict. Every election is a battle for control of the White House and/or both chambers of Congress. Deeply rooted partisanship also explains the growing one-party domination of many states and congressional districts and the remarkable consistency in the results of elections over time and across elected offices. The late House Speaker Tip O'Neill's famous remark that "all politics is local" has been turned on its head. Today, all politics is national.

Deeply rooted partisanship and the close balance between the two major parties at the national level have also helped make divided party control a regular feature of national government. This situation is made even more likely by each party's distinct advantages in different types of elections. Democrats appear to have a growing advantage in presidential elections due to the increasing nonwhite share of the national electorate, which helped move several swing states into the Democratic column between 2000 and 2012. Republicans continue to have an advantage in congressional elections due to the concentration of Democratic voters in urban districts, thanks only in part to Republican control of redistricting in many states. Voters in sparsely populated Republican-leaning states are also overrepresented in the Senate, whose seats cannot be gerrymandered.

Even before the current era of polarized politics, divided party control was a fairly regular occurrence in the decades following World War II. But divided government today has very different consequences. During the 1950s, 1960s, and 1970s, it was much easier to build bipartisan coalitions to pass legislation.[12] There were enough moderate-to-liberal Republicans and moderate-to-conservative Democrats to enable cross-party coalitions on some major issues. Today, however, there are almost no members in the middle in either chamber, and divided party control almost inevitably leads to confrontation and gridlock. With control of both chambers at stake every two years, party leaders in Congress often seem more concerned with posturing and positioning for the next election than with addressing pressing national problems.

The problems of governing in a polarized era have been compounded by the Republican Party's dramatic movement to the right. As Thomas Mann and Norman Ornstein have argued, polarization in Congress is asymmetrical.[13] Since the 1980s, the Republican Party in Congress, and especially in the House of Representatives, has moved much further to the right than the Democratic Party has moved to the left. The rise of the Tea Party movement in 2009 certainly exacerbated this phenomenon, but the GOP's rightward shift was well under way before then.

The growing conservatism of the Republican Party in Congress and in many states reflects the growing conservatism of the Republican electoral base and especially its more active segment.[14] The problem facing Republican leaders and strategists today is that this base is shrinking. The nation is slowly becoming more racially diverse, more secular, and more socially liberal, and these trends are making it more and more difficult for Republican candidates to compete in presidential elections. Even with Donald Trump's Electoral College victory in 2016, Republican candidates have lost the popular vote in six of the last seven presidential elections. But taking the necessary steps to expand the party's appeal to nonwhites and socially liberal Americans would risk deeply offending large segments of the GOP base. This is something few Republican elected officials appear willing to do, especially since few Republican officials need to appeal to these voter groups in order to hold on to their seats.

The forces producing polarization in the American electorate are far from spent. They include, most importantly, the growing racial and ethnic diversity of American society, growing secularism and the decline of traditional religion, and the growing influence of partisan media.[15] Over the short term, and perhaps over the medium term, polarization within the electorate and among political leaders is likely to increase. If this diagnosis is correct, rather than trying to reduce polarization by tinkering with electoral rules and procedures, which is unlikely to prove effective, political scientists and others concerned about the future of American democracy should focus on finding ways to help the political system function in a polarized era.

SIX

White Racial Resentment and the Rise of Donald Trump

Why Trump? This question has baffled political scientists and journalists alike. Donald Trump's success in winning the Republican presidential nomination came as a complete surprise to the vast majority of political observers, including sophisticated data-based journalists like Nate Silver, editor in chief of the news blog FiveThirtyEight, and Nate Cohn of the *New York Times*.[1] For many months after Trump declared his candidacy, and despite his consistently strong showing in both national and early primary state polls, these experts gave the New York real estate mogul and reality TV star almost no chance of winning the nomination.

Journalists are hardly the only ones who were shocked. Trump's victorious primary campaign ran directly counter to the prevailing political science theory of presidential nominations. That theory, known as "the party decides," emphasizes the crucial role of party elites in shaping primary voters' preferences.[2] However, from the day he declared his candidacy until he clinched the nomination, Trump received almost no support from Republican Party leaders and elected officials. Indeed, he was vigorously opposed by much of the party leadership, including its 2008 and 2012 presidential nominees and many of its top elected officials.[3]

In seeking to explain Trump's victory, a number of commentators have focused on rising economic discontent among white, working-class voters adversely affected by the Great Recession and globalization and frustrated with the failure of mainstream Republican leaders to address their concerns. According to this theory, Trump's opposition to free-trade agreements and his promise to bring back lost manufacturing jobs brought strong support from less-educated and lower-income Republican voters.[4] Trump himself, following one of his primary victories, famously bragged about his support from "the poorly educated."[5]

Exit polls of Republican primary voters provide some support for the economic discontent theory. In most states, Trump did somewhat better among less-educated and lower-income voters than among better-educated and higher-income voters—but not always. In Massachusetts, for example, a state with one of the most educated and affluent Republican electorates in the nation, he topped the GOP field with 40 percent of the vote among college graduates, compared with only 24 percent for the second-place finisher, Ohio governor John Kasich. Even more impressively, Trump won 49 percent of the vote among those with household incomes of $100,000 or more, compared with Kasich's 21 percent. A review of data from twenty-three states that held Republican primaries during March and April showed that Trump voters, like other Republican primary voters, had higher incomes and were more likely to be college graduates than the residents of these states and the American public in general. Thus, the economic discontent theory appears to have limited utility for explaining Trump's success. Less-educated Republican voters may have been attracted to Trump's candidacy for reasons other than his economic message.

An alternative explanation of Trump's popularity with Republican primary voters focuses on a different part of his message, a part the candidate himself emphasized from the beginning of his campaign: appeals to white racial fear and resentment.[6] His description of Mexican-American immigrants as criminals and rapists, his repeated promise to build a wall along the Mexican border and make Mexico pay for it, his proposal to deport 11 million undocumented immigrants, his false allegation that thousands of Muslims in New Jersey had celebrated when the twin towers of the World Trade Center came down on September 11, 2001, and his call for a ban on foreign Muslims entering the country were in many ways the centerpiece of his campaign.[7]

Throughout the primary campaign, Trump regularly used his Twitter account to promote messages originating with white supremacists, including the false claim that the majority of white homicide victims in the U.S. in recent years were killed by blacks. He claimed, implausibly, not to know anything about former Ku Klux Klan leader David Duke when asked about Duke's support for his candidacy.[8] Moreover, Trump's use of messages designed to appeal to racial resentment and fear among white voters did not begin with his presidential campaign. He made his first big splash in Republican politics in 2011 as the most prominent promoter of the conspiracy theory known as birtherism—the patently false claim that Barack Obama, the nation's first African-American president, was born not in Hawaii but in Africa and was therefore ineligible to serve as president.[9]

At a time when he was considering a run at the 2012 Republican nomination, Trump's advocacy of birtherism was clearly intended to appeal to the large segment of Republican voters who were upset about the presence of a black man in the White House. Even though he ultimately decided not to run that year, the birther issue clearly worked for Trump. He received enormous media coverage for this outlandish claim, and polling data showed that a large proportion of Republican voters came to question Obama's citizenship and his legitimacy as president.[10] Not surprisingly, given its success, Trump continued to promote this racist conspiracy theory for years, even suggesting that the long-form birth certificate released by the White House in 2011 might be fraudulent.[11]

It is clear that stoking racial fear and resentment was a central element of Trump's strategy during the 2016 Republican primaries. His campaign slogan, "make America great again," emblazoned on his ever-present baseball cap, clearly implied much more than bringing back lost manufacturing jobs. It also signaled voters that a President Trump would turn back the clock to a time when white people enjoyed a dominant position in American society. And in case anyone thought he would change his message after securing the GOP nomination, his decision to put Breitbart News executive Stephen Bannon, one of the leading figures in the white nationalist "alt-right" movement, in charge of his campaign made it clear that appeals to racial resentment would continue even as the candidate "pivoted" to the general election.[12]

There is strong evidence from the 2016 exit polls that Trump's racially tinged fearmongering appealed to a large segment of the Republican primary electorate. In state after state, Republican primary voters who favored deporting undocumented immigrants and banning Muslims from entering the country—two signature Trump positions—favored him by a wide margin over any other candidate. Republicans who opposed these proposals were much less likely to support him. The strength of the relationship between opinions on these issues and support for Trump can be seen in the results of exit polls in four states—Alabama, Michigan, Pennsylvania, and South Carolina. These states represent different regions of the country and held their primaries at different stages of the campaign: South Carolina's contest was one of the earliest, Alabama and Michigan voted in the middle of the campaign, and Pennsylvania came closer to the end, after many of Trump's opponents had dropped out. Nevertheless, across these four states, an average of 52 percent of those who favored deporting all undocumented immigrants voted for Trump, compared with only 32 percent of those who opposed this proposal. Similarly, an average of 52 percent of those who favored a ban on Muslims entering the U.S. voted for Trump, compared with only 20 percent of those who opposed such a ban.

Racial Realignment and the Growth of White Racial Resentment

The exit polls suggest that high levels of racial resentment and fear among a large proportion of Republican voters were crucial to Trump's success in the primaries. Public opinion polls showed that his calls for deportation of undocumented immigrants and a ban on Muslim immigration, along with his proposal to build a wall along the Mexican border and make Mexico pay for it, were quite unpopular among the broader American electorate. However, they resonated strongly with Republican voters. A Pew Research Center poll in August 2016 found that Americans of voting age rejected Trump's proposal for a border wall by 61 percent to 36 percent. But there was a deep party divide on this issue. Democrats and Democratic-leaning independents opposed the wall by an overwhelming margin of 84 percent to 14 percent, while Republicans and Republican-leaning independents favored it by 63 percent to 34 percent.[13]

Trump's success can be seen as an outgrowth of the racial realignment that has transformed the American electorate since the 1970s. For decades before he came on the political scene, Republican elected officials and candidates sought to lure white Democrats into the GOP camp by promoting racially tinged messages about the dangers of African-American crime, forced busing of schoolchildren, and affirmative action, and by emphasizing the complicity

TABLE 6.1. NONWHITE PERCENTAGE OF VOTERS
IN PRESIDENTIAL ELECTIONS, 1976–2012

Year	All voters	Democratic voters	Republican voters
1976	11	15	4
1980	12	23	3
1984	14	29	4
1988	15	26	4
1992	13	21	4
1996	17	25	7
2000	19	29	7
2004	23	34	12
2008	26	40	10
2012	28	45	10

Source: National Exit Polls

of Democratic politicians in these threats. Those efforts clearly paid dividends, helping to elect Republican presidents from Richard Nixon to George W. Bush and to transform the South from the nation's most Democratic region into a Republican stronghold.

As we have seen, between the 1970s and the 2000s the American political system underwent a realignment that transformed the racial, regional, and ideological bases of the major parties. The result was not only a growing gap between the racial compositions of the two electoral coalitions but a dramatic increase in racial resentment among white Republican voters.

Results of national exit polls between 1976 and 2012 show that the racial realignment of the American party system took place in two phases (table 6.1). Following the passage of the Voting Rights Act in 1965, African-Americans surged into the electorate in the southern states, aided by the presence of federal registrars in areas, mainly in the Deep South, where white resistance to black voting rights was the strongest. Black registration rates in the South became comparable to those of whites by about 1976, and the nonwhite share of the electorate in the region and in the nation stabilized at 11 to 15 percent. During this first phase of racial realignment, African-Americans were the great majority of nonwhite voters. As late as 1992, Hispanics and Asian-Americans combined made up only 3 percent of the national electorate.

Between 1976 and 1992, the nonwhite share of Republican voters in presidential elections never rose above 4 percent. The party clearly had very little appeal to African-American voters. The nonwhite share of Democratic voters, meanwhile, varied considerably depending on individual Democratic candidates' appeal to white voters. While Democratic candidates consistently won the overwhelming majority of the African-American vote, their share of the major-party vote among whites ranged from only 34 percent in 1984 to 48 percent in 1976 and 49 percent in 1992. There was a consistent pattern to these results. Moderate southern Democrats like Jimmy Carter and Bill Clinton were much more successful in holding down the Republican margin among white voters than liberal northern Democrats like Walter Mondale and Michael Dukakis. Thus, the racial realignment of the party system appeared to be moving rather slowly and unevenly.

After 1992, however, the pace picked up, mainly because demographic trends were changing the American voting population. Large-scale immigration to the United States from Latin America and Asia between the 1980s and the 2000s, as well as the much younger average age and higher fertility rates of the nonwhite population, caused the nonwhite share of the U.S. population to increase dramatically between the 1980s and the 2000s. Moreover, this trend is expected to continue well into the twenty-first century. And as the population grew more diverse, so, more gradually, did the electorate.

Between 1992 and 2012, the nonwhite share of voters in presidential elections more than doubled, going from 13 percent to 28 percent. However, this growing racial and ethnic diversity had very different effects on the two major parties. The nonwhite share of Republican voters increased modestly between 1992 and 2004, going from 4 percent to 12 percent, mainly due to Republican candidates' ability to attract a sizeable chunk of the growing Hispanic vote. After 2004, however, the nonwhite share of Republican voters fell to 10 percent in both 2008 and 2012, while the nonwhite share of Democratic voters increased steadily—from 21 percent in 1992 to 45 percent in 2012. This trend reflected more than the attraction of the party to nonwhite voters: it also reflected the continued drift of white voters to the GOP, especially in the South. Barack Obama lost the white vote by 20 percentage points, according to the national exit poll in 2012—an astonishing margin, and by far the largest deficit among white voters of any successful Democratic presidential candidate. Yet he won the national popular vote by nearly 4 percentage points due to a margin of 82 to 16 percent among nonwhite voters.

There were two major components to the racial realignment of the U.S. party system between 1992 and 2012—the overwhelming preference of the growing nonwhite voting bloc for the Democratic Party, and the continued movement of white voters from the Democratic to the Republican Party, especially in the South. By 2012, according to data from the ANES, the GOP enjoyed a 55 percent to 39 percent advantage, the highest on record, in leaned party identification among white voters nationwide and an overwhelming 66 percent to 29 percent advantage among white voters in the South.

Several factors helped drive white voters into the Republican camp. Economic issues such as government spending and taxation and cultural issues such as abortion and same-sex marriage clearly played a role in this shift. However, there is no doubt that race played a major role in the realignment of the white electorate. There is clear evidence that as the nation's population and its electorate were be-coming more diverse, a growing number of white voters felt threat-ened by the loss of their dominant status in American society and politics. This can be seen in ANES data on the level of racial re-sentment among white voters.

The concept of racial resentment, as used by social scientists, refers to subtle feelings of hostility toward African-Americans. It is different from old-fashioned racism, which involves beliefs about the white race's inherent superiority and right to dominance. In the ANES survey, the racial-resentment scale is based on how strongly respondents agreed or disagreed with the following assertions:

(1) Irish, Italian, Jewish, and many other minorities overcame prejudice and worked their way up. Blacks should do the same without any special favors.

(2) Generations of slavery and discrimination have created conditions that make it difficult for blacks to work their way out of the lower class.

(3) Over the past few years, blacks have gotten less than they deserve.

(4) It's really a matter of some people not trying hard enough; if blacks would only try harder they could be just as well off as whites.

While these questions focus on attitudes toward African-Americans, scores on the racial-resentment scale correlate highly with feelings toward other racial minorities and out-groups, including recent immigrants.[14]

Data from ANES surveys show that between the Reagan era and the Obama era, there was a marked increase in racial resent-ment among white voters (table 6.2). Over these three decades, the proportion of white voters scoring at the high end of the racial-resentment scale rose from 42 percent to 51 percent. However, this

TABLE 6.2. RACIAL RESENTMENT AMONG WHITE VOTERS
FROM REAGAN TO OBAMA

Presidential era	Racial resentment level			Total	(*n* of cases)
	Low	Moderate	High		
Reagan-Bush 1	27	31	42	100	(1,781)
Clinton	24	32	44	100	(2,113)
Bush 2	23	28	49	100	(1,419)
Obama	22	27	51	100	(1,228)

Note: Percentages should be read horizontally.

Source: American National Election Studies Cumulative File

increase was not uniform. The ANES data show that it was limited to Republican identifiers: racial resentment declined modestly among white Democrats even as it was increasing dramatically among white Republicans (figure 6.1). The proportion of white Republicans scoring at the high end of the racial-resentment scale rose from 44 percent during the Reagan-Bush(1) years to 64 percent during the Obama years.

As recently as the late 1980s, there was little difference in racial resentment between white Democrats and white Republicans. By 2008, however, there was a yawning gap, and it would grow even wider by 2016. It is important to note, however, that racial resentment among white Republicans did not increase only after Barack Obama's emergence on the national political scene in 2008. Instead, it rose steadily over this entire period. It was not Obama who sparked the rise in racial resentment among white Republican voters. Instead, it was the growing visibility and influence of African-Americans and other nonwhites within the Democratic Party, along with ongoing efforts by Republican candidates and strategists to win over racially conservative white voters by portraying Democrats as soft on crime and favoring policies that benefited minorities at the expense of whites.

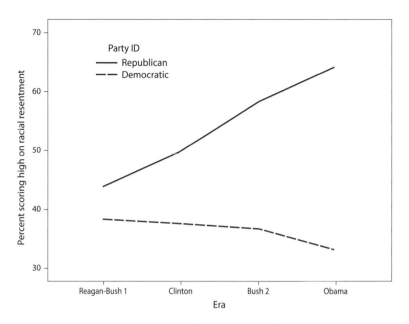

Figure 6.1. Trends in Racial Resentment Among White Democrats and Republicans from Reagan to Obama. (Leaning independents are included with party identifiers.) Source: American National Election Study Cumulative File

There is no way of knowing from the ANES data whether the growing divide between white Democrats and Republicans was due to racially motivated party switching—voters choosing a party based on their racial attitudes—or partisan persuasion: party supporters adopting racial attitudes in response to cues from party leaders. In all likelihood, both forces were at work. Regardless of the direction of influence, however, the end result was a much closer alignment between racial and partisan attitudes among white voters. By the end of the Obama years, racial resentment was pervasive among Republican voters—a situation that would make it much easier for a candidate whose message focused on white racial resentment to win the GOP presidential nomination.

Barack Obama, White Racial Resentment, and the 2008 Election

Barack Obama's emergence on the national political scene in 2008 and his candidacy for the nation's highest office clearly raised the salience of racial issues in that year's election.[15] The impact of racial resentment in an election involving a choice between an African-American candidate and a white one first became evident in the Democratic primary contest between Obama and Hillary Clinton. Even though racial issues were rarely mentioned, and both candidates had similar progressive records and positions on racial issues, the mere presence of an African-American candidate with a real chance of winning the nomination was enough to bring racial resentment into play.

Data from the 2008 ANES show that there was a strong relationship between racial resentment and candidate preference among white voters in the Democratic primaries of that year (table 6.3). In this survey, in addition to the four-item racial resentment scale, respondents were asked whether they had voted in their state's presidential primary or caucus and which candidate they had supported. The results show that racial resentment had a powerful influence on white Democratic primary voters' candidate preferences. About three-fourths of white Democrats who scored at the low end of the racial resentment scale voted for Barack Obama, versus only about one-fourth of those who scored at the high end of the scale.

Certain other characteristics and attitudes were also related to candidate preference. White college graduates were more likely to report voting for Obama than whites without a college degree, as were whites who placed themselves at the liberal end of the ideology scale. In a multivariate analysis, however, the only predictor that continued to have a statistically significant impact was racial resentment. Thus, differences between more and less educated white Democrats, and between more and less liberal Democrats, were

TABLE 6.3. CANDIDATE PREFERENCE OF WHITE VOTERS IN 2008 DEMOCRATIC
PRIMARIES BY SCORE ON RACIAL-RESENTMENT SCALE

	Percentage voting for		
Racial resentment	Obama	Clinton	(*n* of cases)
Very low	74	26	(73)
Low	49	51	(86)
High	36	64	(90)
Very high	26	74	(66)

Source: 2008 American National Election Study

explained largely by differences in racial resentment among these
groups.

Racial resentment affected presidential vote choice in the 2008
general election as well. Despite the overwhelming importance of
partisanship in shaping voters' responses to the presidential candidates, racial resentment still had a significant impact on candidate
preference (table 6.4). Over 90 percent of white Democrats and
Republicans voted for their own party's presidential candidate in
2008. However, partisan defection was substantially higher among
the minority of white Democrats who scored at the high end of the
racial-resentment scale than among those who scored at the low
end. Moreover, among white Republicans, the rate of partisan defection was much greater among the small minority who scored at
the low end of the racial-resentment scale than among those who
scored at the high end. Thus, liberal racial attitudes made Republican voters more receptive to voting for an African-American presidential candidate just as conservative racial attitudes made Democratic voters less receptive.

Even after controlling for party identification, ideology, age, education, and gender, racial resentment had a significant influence
on vote choice in the 2008 presidential election (table 6.5). Party
identification, not surprisingly, was by far the strongest predictor.

TABLE 6.4. PRESIDENTIAL VOTE BY RACIAL RESENTMENT AMONG WHITE
DEMOCRATS AND REPUBLICANS IN 2008

Party ID	Racial resentment	Percentage voting for		(*n* of cases)
		Obama	McCain	
Dem/Lean Dem	Low	97	3	(316)
	Moderate	91	9	(243)
	High	82	18	(226)
Rep/Lean Rep	Low	25	75	(71)
	Moderate	14	86	(171)
	High	6	94	(417)

Source: American National Election Study Cumulative File

However, racial resentment had the second strongest direct influence of any of the independent variables included in this analysis—even stronger than that of ideology. This finding clearly can be attributed to the presence on the ballot of the first African-American nominee of a major party. In presidential elections between 1988

TABLE 6.5. LOGISTIC REGRESSION ANALYSIS OF PRESIDENTIAL VOTE
AMONG WHITES IN 2008

Independent variable	B	Standard error	t-ratio	Sig.
Gender	.203	.200	1.02	N.S.
Age	.011	.005	2.20	.05
Education	.319	.123	2.59	.01
Party ID	.846	.062	13.65	.001
Ideology	.659	.108	6.10	.001
Racial resentment	.227	.030	7.57	.001

Notes: Constant omitted. Dependent variable is vote for McCain vs. Obama. B = Logistic regression coefficient.

Source: American National Election Study Cumulative File

and 2004, racial resentment never had a significant influence on vote choice after controlling for party identification and ideology.

White Racial Resentment and the 2016 Republican Presidential Primary

The influence of racial resentment on candidate choice in a general election is limited by the overwhelming importance of partisanship. In recent years, 90 percent or more of Democratic and Republican identifiers, including leaning independents, have supported their party's nominee. In primary elections, however, party loyalty is not a factor so other influences play a larger role in shaping voters' choices.

Given Donald Trump's reliance on appeals to white racial resentment, the 2016 Republican primaries would appear to provide a clear test of the influence of racial resentment on candidate choice. The American National Election Study Pilot Study of 2016 allows us to examine this question. The Pilot Study was conducted between January 22 and January 28, 2016, just before the Iowa caucuses. By that time, the nomination campaigns had been under way for several months, and the Republican candidates had already had six debates. Most Republican voters had formed a clear preference.

Respondents in the pilot study consisted of twelve hundred voting-age adults who completed an approximately thirty-minute questionnaire online. The sample was designed to be representative of the U.S. voting-age population. Along with the standard demographic, issue, and party identification questions, respondents were asked about their preferences in the Republican and Democratic nomination contests. Most importantly, from our perspective, the four-item racial-resentment scale was administered to all respondents. We can therefore compare the results of the Pilot Study with those of previous ANES national surveys. To permit comparison with earlier ANES surveys, the racial-resentment scale is col-

TABLE 6.6. RACIAL RESENTMENT AMONG WHITE DEMOCRATIC
AND REPUBLICAN VOTERS IN 2016

	Party identification	
Racial resentment	Dem, lean Dem	Rep, lean Rep
Low	50	5
Moderate	31	26
High	19	69
Total	100	100
(*n* of cases)	(225)	(307)

Note: Entries shown are percentages.

Source: 2016 American National Election Study Pilot Survey

lapsed into the same three categories used in the earlier surveys. In addition, to make comparisons over time more meaningful, the analysis is limited to registered voters, and leaning independents are combined with party identifiers.

The data from the Pilot Study show that the divide between white Democrats and Republicans on racial resentment in 2016 was larger than that found in any earlier ANES survey (table 6.6). This reflects both a continued increase in the proportion of Republican voters scoring at the high end of the scale and a sharp drop in the proportion of Democrats scoring at the high end. Between 2008 (the most recent survey including all four racial-resentment items) and 2016, the proportion of white Republican voters scoring at the high end of the scale rose from 64 percent to 69 percent, while white Democratic voters at the high end fell from 33 percent to only 19 percent. This decline in racial resentment among white Democrats was most likely a result of having an African-American Democrat in the White House for the previous seven years.

What is most significant for explaining the rise of Donald Trump is that the Obama years produced an increase in racial resentment among white Republican voters—an increase that came on top of the rather dramatic increase that had occurred previously. The record level of racial resentment among white Republican voters set the stage for Trump's emergence as the frontrunner for the party's presidential nomination.

According to the data from the ANES Pilot Study, in late January, before the Iowa caucuses, Trump already had by far the most support of any candidate for the Republican presidential nomination. Forty percent of registered Republicans named him as their first choice. Senator Ted Cruz of Texas was a distant second at 14 percent, followed by Florida senator Marco Rubio at 12 percent and retired neurosurgeon Ben Carson at 9 percent. Among white Republicans, Trump led Cruz by 44 percent to 15 percent. Among the relatively small group of nonwhite Republicans, Trump received only 19 percent of the vote but still finished first, with Jeb Bush and Rand Paul each receiving 14 percent of the vote.

There was a strong relationship between racial resentment and support for Donald Trump among white Republican voters in the ANES Pilot Study (figure 6.2). For this analysis, I divided racial resentment scores into four categories, ranging from very low to very high: about one-third of white Republicans fell into the lowest category for racial resentment, one-fifth fell into the second lowest category, one-fourth into the second highest category and the remaining fourth into the highest category. The data show that among white Republicans who scored at the low end of the racial-resentment scale, fewer than three in ten favored Trump. In contrast, two-thirds of white Republicans who scored at the high end of the scale favored Trump.

These results suggest that racial resentment had a powerful influence on candidate preference in the 2016 Republican primaries, with the most resentful voters making up a disproportionate share of those attracted to Trump's candidacy. A more definitive test of this hypothesis, however, requires comparing the effect of racial

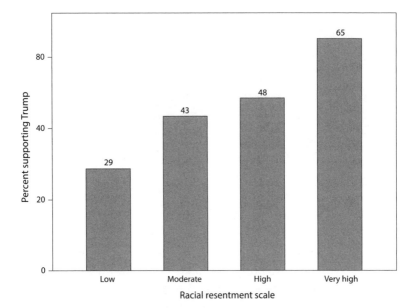

Figure 6.2. Support for Donald Trump by Racial Resentment Among White Republicans in 2016. Source: 2016 American National Election Study Pilot Survey

resentment with the effects of other attitudes and characteristics that might have influenced GOP voters' candidate preferences. For this purpose, I performed a logistic regression analysis of candidate support (table 6.7). The dependent variable in this analysis is support for Trump versus support for any other Republican candidate. The independent variables, along with the racial-resentment scale, are age, gender, education, family income, strength of party identification (coded as 1 for strong Republicans and 0 for weak and independent Republicans), opposition to free-trade agreements, a cultural conservatism scale, and an economic conservatism scale.

The results confirm the findings shown in the previous bar graph illustrating the relationship of scores on the racial-resentment scale

TABLE 6.7. LOGISTIC REGRESSION ANALYSIS OF TRUMP SUPPORT
AMONG WHITE REPUBLICANS IN 2016

Independent variable	B	Standard error	t-ratio	Sig.
Age	.002	.008	0.25	N.S.
Gender/Female	– .179	.277	– 0.65	N.S.
Education	– .135	.089	– 1.52	.10
Income	– .020	.038	– 0.53	N.S.
Strong Republican	.388	.280	1.39	N.S.
Anti-trade	.135	.086	1.57	N.S.
Cultural conservative	– .037	.042	– 0.88	N.S.
Economic conservative	– .120	.044	– 2.73	.01
Racial resentment	.221	.054	4.09	.001

Notes: Constant omitted. Dependent variable is support for Trump vs. any other Republican candidate.

Source: 2016 American National Election Study Pilot Survey

to votes for Trump. Not only did racial resentment have a strong influence on support for Trump, it had by far the strongest influence of any of the independent variables included in the analysis. One other political orientation, economic conservatism, had a statistically significant effect on Trump support: Republicans who were more conservative on economic issues were less likely to support Trump than those who were less conservative. This relationship probably reflects the fact that at various times during the campaign, Trump expressed support for federal programs such as Social Security and Medicare—programs that provided benefits to many of his supporters. However, this effect was considerably weaker than that of racial resentment.

Despite Trump's consistent anti-trade rhetoric, opposition to trade had only a modest and statistically insignificant effect on his support among Republican primary voters. Nor did measures of social class—education and income—have much impact. There was a weak tendency for less educated voters to be more supportive of

Trump, but this relationship did not even reach the .05 level of significance. Family income had essentially no effect. There is no evidence here, after we control for other predictors, that voters who were struggling economically were more likely to support Trump. Much of the apparent relationship between social class and Trump support seems to have been mediated by racial resentment—less-educated and lower-income Republicans were more likely to favor Trump mainly because they tended to have higher levels of racial resentment than those with more education and income.

It Really Was (Mostly) About Race

Donald Trump shocked the American political and media establishment when he captured the Republican presidential nomination in 2016. His win seemed to violate the fundamental laws of presidential nominations, which held that voters follow the lead of party elites. However, Trump's success did not come out of nowhere. Just as Barack Obama's victory in the 2008 Democratic nomination contest reflected fundamental changes in the Democratic electoral coalition, Trump's victory reflected fundamental changes in the Republican electoral coalition, and without these he could never have won the nomination.

The key to Trump's success in the 2016 Republican primaries was the dramatic increase in racial resentment among GOP voters between the 1980s and the 2010s that created a receptive audience for his racial appeals. While Trump was hardly the first Republican presidential candidate to appeal to white racial resentment, the racial content of his messages was far more explicit than those used by earlier GOP candidates like Ronald Reagan and George H. W. Bush. Trump's embrace of the birther myth, his forwarding of tweets from white supremacists, his attacks on Mexican and Muslim immigrants, and his claims of massive voter fraud in African-American communities directly targeted white racial and ethnic fears. Large proportions of GOP primary voters, especially those with less education, responded to these messages, allowing him to win the Republican nomination easily over a divided field of establishment candidates. Moreover, many of these voters would find these messages equally attractive during the general election campaign.

SEVEN

Negative Partisanship and the Triumph of Trump

Donald Trump's victory in the presidential election of 2016 was one of the most shocking upsets in American electoral history. Yet in many ways, it was a direct result of the racial and ideological realignment that has transformed the American electorate since the 1960s. This is not to deny the many highly unusual features of the 2016 presidential campaign. Unpredictable events, such as the letter from FBI director James Comey announcing a renewed investigation into Hillary Clinton's use of a private email server only eleven days before the election and the steady stream of hacked DNC and Clinton campaign email messages released by WikiLeaks, may well have tilted the outcome toward Trump.[1] However, the effects of these events were conditioned by changes in the Republican and Democratic electoral coalitions that long preceded the campaign of 2016.

Deepening racial and ideological divides within the American electorate and a dramatic increase in negative affect toward the opposing party and its leaders made it possible for Trump to win the presidential election despite having the highest negatives of any major party nominee in the history of public opinion polling, and despite losing the national popular vote by a substantial margin. Trump won the Republican nomination over the opposition of virtually the entire GOP establishment by playing to the frustration of much of the Republican electorate, which was angry with the party's leaders for not delivering on clearly unrealistic campaign promises to reverse Barack Obama's policies. That anger was fueled by alarm over changes in American society and culture, including the growing visibility and influence of racial and ethnic minorities.[2]

In the Republican primaries, Trump's reputation as the nation's most prominent advocate of birtherism, his attacks on Mexican immigrants and Muslims, and his promise to "make America great again" by renegotiating trade deals and bringing back lost manufacturing jobs resonated most strongly with white, working-class Republicans. But his appeal was by no means limited to the "poorly educated" or to Republicans. Many racially resentful college-educated Republicans, and even some Democrats, were attracted by Trump's promises to reverse Obama's policies and his attacks on the Washington political establishment.[3] At the same time, however, his racist, xenophobic, and misogynistic comments as well as his attacks on the media and on leaders of both major parties turned off large numbers of voters, especially women and those with college degrees. Even after winning the Republican nomination, Trump's unfavorable ratings remained far higher than his favorable ratings. In fact, for most of 2016 his unfavorable ratings were considerably higher than those of his Democratic opponent, Hillary Clinton.[4]

Two powerful trends contributed greatly to Trump's rise and eventual victory in the presidential election: the politicization of racial resentment among white voters, especially white working-class voters, and the rise of negative partisanship. Both trends reflected the growing alignment of partisanship with race, religion, and ideology—a transformation described in previous chapters of this book. More than any other presidential candidate in recent history, Trump effectively exploited the racial, cultural, and ideological divisions in the electorate by directly appealing to white racial hostility and by demonizing the opposing party's nominee. His strategy clearly influenced shifts in voting patterns between 2012 and 2016.

The Political Geography of the 2016 Election

We have seen that the geographic bases of the Democratic and Republican parties have changed dramatically since the 1970s, and that this transformation has largely reflected the growing alignment of partisanship with ideology.[5] Because of this growing alignment, states with relatively conservative electorates, including many in the Mountain West and the South, have trended strongly toward the Republican Party, while states with relatively liberal electorates, including many in the Northeast and on the Pacific Coast, have trended strongly Democratic.[6] There have been some changes in voter ideology in the states as well, but the biggest shifts have involved partisanship. Some states that supported Democratic presidential candidates as recently as 1996, like Arkansas, West Virginia, and Louisiana, are now among the most reliably Republican states in the nation. Meanwhile, a number of states that supported Republican presidential candidates as recently as 1988, like California, Connecticut, New Jersey, and Vermont, are now among the most reliably Democratic.

The growing alignment of state partisanship with state ideology has brought growing stability to geographic voting patterns from election to election as well as a decline in the number of battleground states. In the four presidential elections between 2000 and 2012, forty of the fifty states along with the District of Columbia consistently supported the same party. Over these four elections, the number of states decided by a margin of less than 5 percentage points fell from twelve in 2000 to only four in 2012, while the number of states decided by at least 15 percentage points rose from twenty-three to thirty. Growing partisan polarization among the voters was accompanied by growing polarization among the states.

Much of the commentary about the results of the 2016 presidential election has focused on the shifts in voting patterns, including geographic voting patterns, which enabled Donald Trump to win the electoral vote. Indeed, there were some significant shifts at the state level between 2012 and 2016. Six states swung from the Democratic column to the Republican column: Florida, Pennsylvania, Ohio, Michigan, Wisconsin, and Iowa. Two of these states, Pennsylvania and Michigan, had not supported a Republican presidential candidate since 1988, and one, Wisconsin, had not supported one since 1984. Trump's narrow victories in these three states, which had been considered key parts of a Democratic "blue wall," were perhaps the most shocking aspect of the results for Democratic leaders and strategists.[7] However, these three states switching sides was not the only important shift between 2012 and 2016.

A closer examination of the results of the 2016 presidential election at the state level shows that despite some important shifts, voting patterns between 2012 and 2016 showed a great deal of continuity. A scatterplot of the Trump margin in 2016 versus the Romney margin in 2012 across all fifty states and the District of Columbia shows that, in general, Trump received his largest margins in the same states where Romney received his largest margins, and Clinton received her largest margins in the same states where Obama received his largest margins (figure 7.1). The correlation of .94 between Trump's margin in 2016 and Romney's in 2012 is quite impressive considering that these two elections involved completely different candidates. And the correlation jumps to .97 if we exclude one state—Utah—where a conservative Mormon Republican

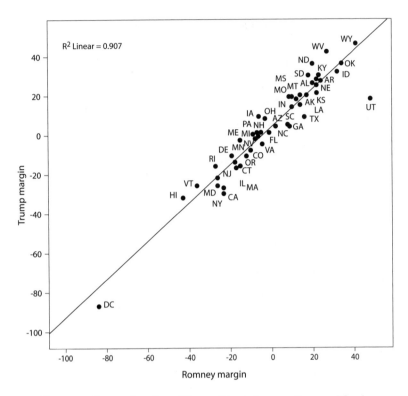

Figure 7.1. Scatterplot of 2016 Trump Margin by 2012 Romney Margin
in the States. Source: uselectionatlas.org

running as an independent, Evan McMullen, took 22 percent of the
vote.

There were more closely contested states in 2016 than four years
earlier—eleven states, with 134 electoral votes, were decided by a
margin of less than 5 percentage points compared with four states
with only 75 electoral votes in 2012. However, there were just as
many blowout states in 2012 as in 2016—nineteen states and the
District of Columbia, with 187 electoral votes, were decided by 20
points or more. Another fourteen states with 116 electoral votes

Table 7.1. States with Largest Shifts in Vote Margins
Between 2012 and 2016

States with Republican shift		States with Democratic shift	
North Dakota	+ 16	Utah	+ 30
Iowa	+ 15	California	+ 7
West Virginia	+ 15	Texas	+ 7
Maine	+ 12	Arizona	+ 5
South Dakota	+ 12	Massachusetts	+ 4
Ohio	+ 11	Georgia	+ 3
Hawaii	+ 11	District of Columbia	+ 3
Rhode Island	+ 11	Virginia	+ 1
Vermont	+ 10	Washington	+ 1
Michigan	+ 9	Kansas	+ 1
Indiana	+ 9		
Missouri	+ 9		
Wisconsin	+ 8		
Delaware	+ 8		

Source: uselectionatlas.org

were decided by a margin of 10 to 20 percentage points. Thus the results in thirty-three states and the District of Columbia, with a total of 303 electoral votes, were never in doubt—much more than in earlier nationally competitive elections such as 1960 or 1976.

Despite this high degree of continuity, several states saw large shifts in support. Moreover, these swings moved in opposing directions (table 7.1). At the national level, there was a modest Republican swing of less than 2 percentage points—from a 3.9-point Democratic margin in 2012 to a 2.1-point Democratic margin in 2016. However, fifteen states saw a Republican swing of at least 8 points, and ten states experienced a Democratic swing of at least 1 point.

Some of the largest swings can be attributed to idiosyncratic factors. The 30-point Democratic swing in Utah clearly reflected both the extraordinary popularity of the Republican nominee in 2012 and the extraordinary unpopularity of the Republican nominee in 2016 with Mormon voters, along with the presence on the 2016 ballot of an independent Mormon candidate from Utah. The 11-point Republican swing in Hawaii can be attributed to Barack Obama's unique appeal to voters in his native state, and the 10-point Republican swing in Vermont can be attributed to a large write-in vote for that state's senator, Bernie Sanders, after his unsuccessful bid for the Democratic nomination.

Beyond these idiosyncratic factors, however, there was a pattern to the movement between the two elections. A number of the states where Donald Trump did exceptionally well compared with Mitt Romney are in the Northeast and Midwest, including the battleground states of Iowa, Ohio, Michigan, and Wisconsin. These states all have relatively low proportions of nonwhites and relatively large proportions of white working-class voters. Many of the states where Hillary Clinton did better than Barack Obama, such as California, Texas, Arizona, and Georgia, have relatively large and growing proportions of nonwhites and relatively small proportions of white working-class voters.

In an effort to explain vote shifts in the states between 2012 and 2016, I conducted a multiple regression analysis using the 2016 Trump margin as the dependent variable. The independent variables in this analysis included the 2012 Romney margin, the percentage of college graduates in the adult population, the percentage of African-Americans in the population, the percentage of Hispanics in the population, and the percentage of Mormons in the population (table 7.2).

In order to determine whether state economic conditions had any effect on vote shifts, I included a measure of state unemployment in November 2016 from the Bureau of Labor Statistics. In addition, in order to determine whether the campaigns had any impact on vote shifts, I included a dummy variable for the twelve swing

TABLE 7.2. REGRESSION ANALYSIS OF 2016 TRUMP MARGIN IN THE STATES

Independent variable	Beta	t-ratio	Significance
Romney margin	.836	22.62	.001
College grads	–.180	–4.94	.001
African-American	–.093	–3.77	.001
Hispanic	–.132	–5.72	.001
Mormon	–.166	–6.75	.001
Unemployment	–.020	–0.77	N.S.
Swing state	–.013	–0.36	N.S.
Trump rallies	.005	0.05	N.S.
Clinton rallies	.007	0.07	N.S.
Adjusted R^2 = .98			

Source: Data compiled by author

states along with counts of the numbers of Trump and Clinton rallies held in each swing state based on data gathered by NBC News. Coefficients displayed in this table are standardized regression coefficients, or beta weights, which make it possible to directly compare the effects of the various predictors.

The results of the regression analysis show that across all fifty states and the District of Columbia, the 2012 Romney margin was by far the strongest predictor of the 2016 Trump margin. This finding reinforces the point that despite some substantial shifts in the results at the state level, geographic voting patterns showed a great deal of continuity between these two elections. The data did show, however, that several demographic factors played major roles in producing shifts at the state level. These demographic variables, along with the 2012 results, explain almost all of the variance in state election margins in 2016.

First, not surprisingly, states with larger Mormon populations tended to shift toward the Democrats. This was largely due to the dramatic decline in the Republican margin in Utah, where Evan

McMullen, the independent candidate, received over 22 percent of the vote. The only other state where he received more than 3 percent of the vote was Idaho—the state with the second largest proportion of Mormons in the nation.

Three other demographic variables had substantial and highly statistically significant effects on vote shifts in the states. The larger the proportion of college graduates, the larger the proportion of African-Americans, and the larger the proportion of Hispanics in a state's population, the larger the shift toward Hillary Clinton (or the smaller the shift toward Donald Trump). These findings underline the crucial role played by the white working class in Trump's victory. States in which Trump outperformed Romney had lower racial and ethnic diversity and lower levels of education compared with states in which he underperformed Romney. One of the keys to Trump's Electoral College victory was that all of the battleground states in the Midwest and Northeast—Michigan, Wisconsin, Pennsylvania, Ohio, and Iowa—have less racially diverse and less educated electorates than the national average.[8]

The regression results also show that economic and campaign-related variables had little or no effect. Compared to Romney, Trump did no better in states with relatively high unemployment than in those with relatively low unemployment. He did no better in swing states than in non-swing states. Moreover, the numbers of campaign rallies held by Trump and Clinton in the swing states had no apparent impact. Trump held more campaign rallies than Clinton in every swing state except Virginia, where neither candidate held a rally. But there is no evidence here that Trump's success in the swing states was due to his rallies, or that Clinton would have performed better if she had held more rallies in these states. The fact that Clinton held fewer rallies than Trump in Pennsylvania, Michigan, and Wisconsin—she famously never visited Wisconsin—probably does not explain why she narrowly lost all of those states.

Trump's margin in each of these states was very close to what would be predicted based entirely on the state's 2012 Romney margin and its demographic profile.

The Revolt of the White Working Class

The main conclusion from the results of the regression analysis of state election results—that compared with Mitt Romney, Trump did best in states with less racially diverse and less educated electorates—is reinforced by the results from the 2012 and 2016 national exit polls (table 7.3). According to the national exit poll, Trump won the white vote by about 20 points, almost the same margin as Romney. However, just as there were shifts in opposing directions in the states, there were shifts in opposing directions among voters, particularly white voters. Republican support rose among white men but fell among white women. Trump's well publicized misogynistic comments, his bragging about inappropriate sexual advances on the notorious *Access Hollywood* tape, and accusations of sexual assault by various women undoubtedly hurt him with female voters. Nevertheless, he still outpolled Hillary Clinton by 9 percentage points among white women, according to the national exit poll. Moreover, he made up for his losses among white women by defeating Clinton by close to a two-to-one margin among white men.

The opposing swings among white college graduates and non-graduates are even more striking than the opposing swings among white women and men. Among white college graduates, Trump's 3-point margin was the smallest in decades, far smaller than Romney's 14-point margin in 2012. Among white voters without college degrees, however, his 37-point margin was 12 points larger than Romney's.

Among white voters in 2016, the class divide was much larger than the gender divide. Trump defeated Clinton by 61 percent to 34 percent among white working-class women and by a remarkable

TABLE 7.3. CHANGE IN REPUBLICAN MARGIN AMONG WHITE VOTER GROUPS
BETWEEN 2012 AND 2016

Voter group	Republican margin in		Change
	2012	2016	
Male	+ 27	+ 31	+ 4
Female	+ 14	+ 9	− 5
College grads	+ 14	+ 3	− 11
Non-grads	+ 25	+ 37	+ 12

Source: National Exit Polls

71 percent to 23 percent among white working-class men. However, his margin among white male college graduates was much narrower, 53 percent to 39 percent, and he lost to Clinton among white female college graduates by 51 percent to 44 percent.

White working-class voters have been moving toward the Republican Party since at least the 1970s, but the shift toward Trump in 2016 was truly remarkable. It is what gave Trump his narrow victories in Michigan, Pennsylvania, and Wisconsin. While the size of this group has been shrinking for decades, it continues to make up a large share of the American electorate, especially in the swing states of the Northeast and Midwest. A crucial question for anyone trying to understand the results of the 2016 election, therefore, is why Trump's candidacy was so appealing to white working-class voters even as it repelled large numbers of white college graduates along with the vast majority of nonwhite voters.

As I discussed in Chapter 6, explanations for Trump's appeal to Republican primary voters generally focused on two sets of factors. One explanation emphasized the role of economic discontent and anxiety. According to this hypothesis, Trump's attacks on trade deals such as NAFTA and his promise to bring back good jobs in manufacturing and mining appealed strongly to white voters in small to medium-sized cities and rural areas that had been hard hit by the Great Recession and had not seen as strong a recovery as larger metropolitan areas.[9] The second explanation emphasizes racial and ethnic fears and resentment. This hypothesis focuses on Trump's early embrace of birtherism, his explicit attacks on immigrants and Muslims, and his retweeting of messages and reluctance to disavow support from prominent white nationalist leaders and groups.[10]

Of course, these two explanations are not mutually exclusive. Both may have some validity. Moreover, as Michael Tesler has argued, economic discontent among white voters in 2016 appears to have been closely connected to racial resentment. His analysis of survey data indicates that many white voters, especially those without college degrees, believe that racial minorities and immigrants have been favored by government policies while their own communities have been neglected, especially during the Obama years.[11] The Trump campaign explicitly connected these issues by arguing that illegal immigrants were taking jobs away from American citizens and reducing wages for American workers.

We have already seen that racial resentment was the single strongest predictor of support for Trump among Republican primary voters. It seems reasonable to expect that racial resentment was also an important predictor in the general election. However, this still leaves us with an important question: what might explain the extraordinary level of support for Trump among white voters without college degrees compared with their support for earlier Republican presidential candidates? After all, this group was known to harbor strong feelings of racial resentment long before Donald Trump entered politics.

One possible explanation for Trump's surge among these voters is that, compared with previous GOP presidential candidates, he made a much more explicit appeal to white racial resentment. Thus his campaign may have helped to politicize racial resentment, espe-

TABLE 7.4. CORRELATIONS OF RACIAL-RESENTMENT SCALE WITH
PRESIDENTIAL CANDIDATE FEELING THERMOMETER DIFFERENCE RATINGS
BY EDUCATION AMONG WHITE VOTERS, 1988–2016

Year	All white voters	College grads	Not college grads
1988	.205	.308	.175
1992	.275	.510	.157
2000	.247	.398	.154
2004	.398	.628	.261
2008	.485	.611	.416
2016	.636	.699	.549

Sources: American National Election Study Cumulative File and 2016 American National Election Study

cially among less-educated white voters, who tend to be less attentive to political campaigns and therefore less aware of differences between candidates.[12] To test this hypothesis, we can compare the correlations between scores on the racial-resentment scale and relative ratings of the Republican and Democratic presidential candidates on the feeling thermometer scale over time among white voters with and without college degrees (table 7.4). Data are available for all elections between 1988, when the ANES first began asking the questions in the racial resentment scale, and 2016, except for 2012 when the ANES survey did not include all four of the racial resentment items.

The results show that the politicization of racial resentment among white voters began well before 2016. As expected, this relationship has consistently been stronger among white college graduates than among whites without college degrees. In 2008, however, the presence of an African-American candidate on the presidential ballot led to a sharp increase in the correlation between racial resentment and feeling thermometer ratings among white working-class voters. Data from the 2016 ANES indicate that Trump's heavy

Year	All white voters	College grads	Not college grads
1988	+23	+35	+18
1992	+28	+44	+17
2000	+27	+45	+14
2004	+42	+64	+27
2008	+52	+61	+50
2016	+69	+73	+63

Sources: American National Election Study Cumulative File and 2016 American National Election Study

emphasis on racial issues further strengthened this relationship, especially among white voters without college degrees. In terms of shared variance, the relationship between racial resentment and candidate feeling thermometer ratings was about 2.6 times stronger in 2016 than in 2004 among all white voters, but it was more than 4 times stronger among white working-class voters.

What ultimately matters, of course, is how these feelings translate into votes. I therefore analyzed the relationship between the racial resentment scale and presidential voting decisions in every election since 1988 for which the ANES survey included the full racial-resentment scale by comparing the difference between the Republican share of the major-party vote among whites scoring at the high end of the racial-resentment scale and those scoring at the low end (table 7.5). A positive score indicates that those scoring at the high end of the scale were more likely to report voting for the Republican candidate than those scoring at the low end of the scale.

The results of this analysis are entirely consistent with the trends in the correlation coefficients. Over time, the difference in support for the Republican presidential candidate between whites scoring at the high and low ends of the racial-resentment scale has increased dramatically. Almost all of this increase has occurred since 2000. Once again, although the relationship between racial resentment and candidate choice has strengthened considerably among both college and non-college whites, since 2004 the increase has been greater among whites without a college degree. Among white voters with college degrees in 2004, the gap in support for the Republican candidate between those scoring high and low on the racial resentment scale was 64 percentage points, while the gap among white voters without college degrees was only 27 percentage points. In 2016, however, the gap among white voters with college degrees was 73 percentage points and the gap among white voters without college degrees was 63 percentage points.

These results reflect the fact that over the past four elections, there has been a dramatic increase in support for Republican presidential candidates among the most racially resentful white working-class voters. In 2000, only 62 percent of working-class whites scoring high on racial resentment voted for George W. Bush over Al Gore. The Republican candidate's share increased slightly to 68 percent in 2004 and 69 percent in 2008. In 2016, however, 87 percent of the most racially resentful white working-class voters supported Donald Trump over Hillary Clinton. Meanwhile, among the least racially resentful white working-class voters, the Republican share of the major party vote actually fell, from 48 percent in 2000 and 41 percent in 2004 to 19 percent in 2008 and 24 percent in 2016.

Trump's 2016 campaign included frequent appeals to white voters who were upset about economic trends such as stagnant wages and the loss of manufacturing jobs. What was most striking about his campaign, however, was how he explicitly invoked white resentment over the increasing visibility and influence of racial and ethnic minorities. Moreover, he connected these two issues by blaming economic problems on bad trade deals with countries like Mexico and China and on immigrants' competing for jobs.

TABLE 7.6. POLITICAL AND ECONOMIC ATTITUDES OF COLLEGE GRADUATES
AND NON-COLLEGE GRADUATES AMONG WHITE VOTERS IN 2016

	College grads	Non-college
Rate Trump higher on feeling thermometer	41	61
High racial/ethnic resentment	27	50
High misogyny	29	51
National economy worse	23	36
Family finances worse	21	30
Less economic mobility	67	72
Oppose free trade deals	15	27

Note: Entries shown are percentages.

Source: 2016 American National Election Study

According to the 2016 exit poll, Trump's appeals to discontented white voters resonated most strongly among those without college degrees. The data from the 2016 American National Election Study show the same pattern (table 7.6). According to the ANES data, Trump won 66 percent of the vote among white voters without college degrees compared with only 44 percent of the vote among white college graduates. Moreover, white voters without college degrees were much more likely than white college graduates to agree with key elements of Trump's campaign message.

Compared with college graduates, white voters without college degrees were more much more likely to score high on measures of racial and ethnic resentment and misogyny.[13] They were also somewhat more likely to hold negative views of economic conditions, to view economic mobility as less possible than in the past, and to oppose free-trade deals—although these differences were generally smaller, and relatively few whites with or without college degrees were opposed to free-trade agreements.

To compare the impact of racial and ethnic resentment with that of economic discontent, I conducted a multiple regression analysis

TABLE 7.7. REGRESSION ANALYSIS OF TRUMP-CLINTON FEELING THERMOMETER
RATINGS AMONG WHITE VOTERS IN 2016

Independent variable	Beta	t-ratio	Significance
Party identification	.433	23.7	.001
Ideology	.062	3.3	.001
Age	.027	2.2	.025
Gender	.023	1.9	.05
Education	.003	0.3	N.S.
Resentment	.319	17.8	.001
Misogyny	.071	5.2	.001
Free trade	.061	4.8	.001
Family finances	.022	1.7	.05
National economy	.151	10.1	.001
Economic mobility	.035	2.9	.01
Adjusted R^2 = .76			

Source: 2016 American National Election Study

of relative feeling thermometer ratings of Trump and Clinton among white voters using the data from the ANES survey (table 7.7). Relative feeling thermometer ratings provide a more nuanced measure of vote choice. Still, these ratings strongly predict vote choice: only 3 percent of white voters rated Trump and Clinton equally on the feeling thermometer, and 97 percent of those rating one candidate higher reported voting for that candidate. In addition to the measures of racial/ethnic resentment and economic discontent discussed above, I included several control variables in the regression analysis, including party identification, ideology, age, education, and gender.

The variables included in the regression analysis explain over three-fourths of the variance in feeling thermometer ratings of Trump and Clinton. After party identification, racial/ethnic resentment was by far the strongest predictor: the higher the score on the racial/ethnic resentment scale, the more favorably white voters rated Trump relative to Clinton. The impact of the racial/ethnic resentment scale was much stronger than that of any of the economic variables included in the analysis, including opinions about free-trade deals and economic mobility. Moreover, the effect of racial/ethnic resentment was much stronger than that of ideology. Among the measures of economic discontent, ratings of the national economy had the strongest influence: the more negative the rating of the economy, the more positively white voters rated Trump relative to Clinton. Other measures of economic discontent had relatively weak effects.

After we control for the other variables, the impact of education on relative ratings of Trump and Clinton completely disappears. The difference between white voters with and without college degrees in support for Trump is almost entirely explained by racial/ethnic resentment. An examination of the relationship between scores on the racial/ethnic resentment scale and support for Trump among white voters with and without college degrees shows that regardless of education, there was a very strong relationship between racial/ethnic resentment and support for Trump (figure 7.2). Moreover, there was almost no difference between white voters with and without college degrees after controlling for racial/ethnic resentment. White voters with high levels of racial/ethnic resentment voted overwhelmingly for Trump regardless of education, and white voters with low levels of racial/ethnic resentment voted overwhelmingly for Clinton regardless of education.

Ratings of the national economy had a substantial impact on white voters' relative ratings of Trump and Clinton after we control for all of the other predictors in the regression analysis, including racial/ethnic resentment. What these results do not make clear, however, is that there was a close connection among white voters between racial resentment and economic discontent. Fifty percent of those scoring "very high" or "high" on the racial/ethnic discon-

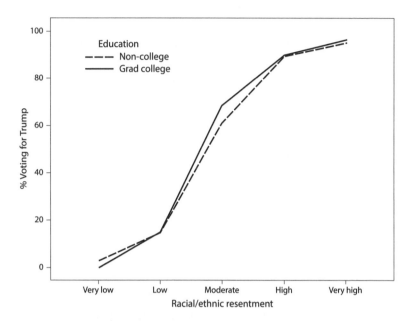

Figure 7.2. Percentage Voting for Trump by Racial/Ethnic Resentment
Among College and Non-College Whites in 2016.
Source: 2016 American National Election Study

tent scale rated economic conditions as worse than one year earlier, compared with only six percent of those scoring "low" or "very low."

While these cross-sectional survey data do not tell us the direction of influence between these two variables, there are good theoretical reasons to believe that racial resentment has a stronger influence on economic discontent than the reverse. For one thing, racial attitudes are generally more stable than assessments of economic conditions, which can fluctuate considerably, even over a short time. Moreover, the Trump campaign directly connected white workers' job losses with government policies favoring nonwhites and immigrants.

Intra-Party Polarization in the 2016 Electorate

Donald Trump did not run for president as a traditional conservative. During both the Republican primaries and the general election campaign, he took several positions that went against conservative orthodoxy.[14] He promised not to cut spending on the two largest federal entitlement programs, Social Security and Medicare, and he promised a massive increase in federal spending on infrastructure projects. He attacked trade deals like NAFTA and the Trans-Pacific Partnership (TPP), which were popular with economic conservatives and their allies in the business community but unpopular with many union leaders and members.[15]

Trump's unorthodox positions on these issues and his strong appeal to white working-class voters raise an important question. Did his candidacy attract support from voters whose ideological orientations and policy preferences differed noticeably from those of traditional Republican voters? To address this question, I compared the views of voters who supported Trump in the GOP primary with the views of voters who supported other Republican candidates on a wide range of issues included in the 2016 ANES Pilot Study that was conducted in late January. I did a similar comparison for voters supporting Hillary Clinton and Bernie Sanders in the Democratic primary. Just as Trump's success in the GOP primaries shocked Republican Party leaders, the success of Sanders in the Democratic primaries shocked the Democratic establishment. Even though Sanders ultimately failed to win the Democratic nomination, his strong showing among younger and more liberal voters exposed important divisions within the Democratic electorate.[16]

Data from the ANES Pilot Study comparing the liberalism of Democratic and Republican voters on a variety of issues depending on their primary candidate preference show that, for the most part, Trump supporters and supporters of other GOP candidates did not

Table 7.8. Policy Polarization in 2016: Liberalism of Republican and Democratic Voters by Primary Candidate Preference

Issue	Identify/Lean Republican		Identify/Lean Democratic	
	Favor Trump	Favor other	Favor Clinton	Favor Sanders
Ideological identification	3	5	59	80
Child care spending	28	20	73	80
Government services	10	10	72	79
Health insurance spending	28	24	87	87
Minimum wage	34	23	82	92
Climate change	37	20	83	90
Employer birth control exemption	29	27	78	92
Same-sex wedding exemption	16	16	59	72
Immigration	39	62	77	82
Average liberalism	25	23	74	84

Note: Entries shown are percentages.

Source: 2016 American National Election Study Pilot Survey

differ much on policy (table 7.8). On two issues, climate change and the minimum wage, Trump voters were somewhat more liberal than those favoring other candidates. Even there, however, the large majority of Trump voters came down on the conservative side. But on one issue, Trump supporters were substantially more conservative than supporters of other GOP candidates: immigration. This question asked whether respondents thought the number of legal immigrants allowed into the United States should be increased, decreased, or left unchanged. Sixty-one percent of Republicans supporting Trump favored decreasing the number of legal immigrants allowed in the country, compared with only 38 percent of those supporting other Republican candidates.

The data from the Pilot Study show that on some issues, differences among Democrats were larger than differences among Republicans. For example, Sanders supporters were more likely than Clinton supporters to oppose allowing religious organizations to opt out of providing contraceptive coverage under the Affordable Care Act and to oppose allowing businesses providing wedding services to refuse to serve same-sex couples. Moreover, 80 percent of Sanders supporters identified themselves as liberal compared with only 59 percent of Clinton supporters. Still, on most issues the differences between Sanders and Clinton supporters were quite small.

The main conclusion one can draw from the evidence from the Pilot Study is that the policy differences between Democrats and Republicans were far greater than those between supporters of different candidates within each party. On every one of these issues, the large majority of Democrats supporting Clinton and the large majority of Democrats supporting Sanders came down on the liberal side, while the large majority of Republicans supporting Trump and the large majority of Republicans supporting other candidates came down on the conservative side. On average, 78 percent of Democratic voters took the liberal side on these issues compared with only 24 percent of Republican voters. Based on these findings, it appears that Trump's candidacy did little to alter the fundamental ideological divide between Democrats and Republicans.

Issue Constraint and Ideological Thinking in 2016

Data from the ANES Pilot Study on the policy preferences of registered voters also showed a high degree of consistency in responses to different policy issues. Across nine questions included in the survey, the average inter-item correlation was a very impressive .45, and the average correlation among opinions on the five economic issues—government services, health care spending, child care spending, the minimum wage, and climate change—was an even more impressive .62.

The average correlation between the ideological identification question and the eight specific policy questions was .50, which is also strong. Moreover, the average correlation between the five economic issues and the two cultural issues—allowing exemptions for religious organizations from the ACA's contraceptive coverage mandate, and allowing businesses providing wedding services to refuse service to same-sex couples—was a solid .41, an impressive level of consistency for opinions in different policy domains. These correlations, in fact, were just as strong as those found by Philip Converse among political elites in his classic study of elite and mass belief systems.[17] The level of issue constraint found in this survey clearly suggests that ideological thinking was quite prevalent in the 2016 electorate. Opinions on economic issues were closely related to opinions on cultural issues, and opinions on both types of issues were closely related to ideological self-placement.

Affective Polarization and Negative Partisanship in 2016

One of the most important developments in American public opinion over the past thirty years has been the rise of affective polarization. Democrats and Republicans are increasingly divided not just in their policy preferences but in their increasingly negative feelings about the opposing party and its leaders.[18] This has given rise to the phenomenon of negative partisanship: large proportions of Democrats and Republicans now dislike the opposing party more than they like their own. Dislike of the other side is so strong, in fact, that even when partisans have deep reservations about their own party's candidate, they are very reluctant to cross party lines. The result, as we have seen, is record levels of party loyalty and straight-ticket voting.[19]

The presidential election of 2016 set new records for affective polarization and negative partisanship. Both major party nominees had exceptionally high unfavorable ratings. According to the Gallup

Poll, Trump had the highest unfavorable ratings of any presidential candidate in modern history. Clinton was not far behind.[20] However, this does not mean that most voters disliked both candidates. According to Gallup, only about one out of four Americans disliked both.[21] Most Democratic voters had a favorable opinion of Clinton and most Republican voters had a favorable opinion of Trump. It is true that many Republican voters had reservations about Trump and quite a few Democratic voters had reservations about Hillary Clinton. But vast majorities on both sides strongly preferred their party's nominee because they intensely disliked the opposing party's nominee.[22]

Both Trump and Clinton went through long and divisive battles for their party's nomination. Clinton was viewed as a strong favorite from the outset but had to fend off a surprisingly strong challenge from the left by Senator Bernie Sanders of Vermont. Trump shocked almost everyone by winning the nomination rather easily over a crowded field of politically experienced Republican candidates. Even though he led in polls of Republican voters from the moment he announced his candidacy, Trump ended up winning less than half of the vote in the primaries. For both candidates, therefore, one of the biggest challenges in the general election campaign was winning over voters who had supported other candidates in the primaries.

Despite the divisiveness of the Democratic and Republican nomination contests and their own high unfavorable ratings, in the end both Clinton and Trump largely succeeded in uniting their party's voters in the general election. According to the national exit poll, party loyalty in the 2016 presidential election was about as high as in other recent presidential elections: almost 89 percent of Democratic identifiers and 88 percent of Republican identifiers voted for their own party's nominee. Only 8 percent of Democratic and Republican identifiers defected to the opposing party's nominee, while

TABLE 7.9. AFFECTIVE POLARIZATION IN 2016: AVERAGE FEELING
THERMOMETER RATINGS OF CLINTON AND TRUMP BY PARTY
AND PRIMARY CANDIDATE PREFERENCE

	Clinton	Trump	Difference
Identify/Lean Democratic	70.9	18.9	+ 52.0
Favor Clinton	86.8	20.4	+ 66.4
Favor Sanders	55.5	13.6	+ 41.9
Identify/Lean Republican	12.5	65.0	− 52.5
Favor Trump	11.4	90.8	− 79.4
Favor other	12.6	49.9	− 37.3

Source: 2016 ANES Pilot Study

3 percent of Democratic identifiers and 4 percent of Republican identifiers voted for third-party candidates.

The key to Trump's and Clinton's success in uniting their party's voters was negative partisanship. A comparison of the average feeling thermometer ratings of Trump and Clinton by Democratic and Republican voters supporting different primary candidates in the 2016 ANES Pilot Study shows that among all Republican voters, Donald Trump received an average rating of 65 degrees (table 7.9). Among all Democratic voters, Hillary Clinton received an average rating of 71 degrees. These are mediocre ratings for presidential nominees from their own party's voters. In 2012, Barack Obama received an average rating of 82 degrees from Democratic voters and Mitt Romney an average of 72 degrees from Republican voters. However, ratings of the opposing party's candidate were far more negative in 2016 than in 2012. In 2012, Obama received an average rating of 29 degrees from Republican voters while Mitt Romney received an average rating of 28 degrees from Democratic voters. In 2016, however, Republican voters gave Hillary Clinton an average rating of 12 degrees and Democratic voters gave Donald Trump an average rating of 19 degrees.

These results show that among both Democrats and Republicans there was a large gap in feelings toward the party's nominee between voters who supported the nominee in the primaries and voters who supported other primary candidates. Republican voters who supported Trump in the primaries gave him an average rating of 91 degrees, while those who supported other candidates rated him only 50 degrees. Democratic voters who supported Clinton in the primaries gave her an average rating of 87 degrees, while her rating from Sanders supporters averaged just 58 degrees.

Yet the vast majority of voters who supported other candidates in the primaries rated Clinton and Trump more favorably than the opposing party's nominee. Eighty-eight percent of Sanders supporters rated Clinton higher than Trump on the feeling thermometer, versus just 8 percent who rated her lower; and 82 percent of Republicans supporting candidates other than Trump rated him higher than Clinton, with only 12 percent rating her more favorably. The reason for this is clear from the data on average feeling thermometer ratings shown in the preceding table: Sanders supporters disliked Trump even more than Clinton supporters did. They gave him an average rating of only 14 degrees on the feeling thermometer. Republicans supporting primary candidates other than Trump disliked Clinton almost as much as those supporting Trump, giving her an average rating of 13 degrees.

It is striking that these intensely negative feelings toward the opposing party's eventual nominee were measured in January of 2016. This was long before Trump and Clinton emerged as their party's presidential nominees and began what many political observers described as one of the nastiest and most negative campaigns in modern political history. According to these data, Democratic and Republican voters did not need to be persuaded to despise the opposing party's candidate. Most Republicans strongly disliked Clinton and most Democrats strongly disliked Trump long before the general election campaign began. For most voters, the general election campaign served mainly to reinforce the extremely negative feelings they had long held toward the opposing party's nominee.

How Polarization and Negative Partisanship Helped Trump Win

Because they so intensely disliked the opposing party's nominee, even voters who had serious reservations about their own party's nominee were very reluctant to cross party lines. Donald Trump was unacceptable to the vast majority of Democrats, including those who had supported Sanders in the Democratic primaries. Hillary Clinton was unacceptable to the vast majority of Republicans, even those who had opposed Trump in the primaries. However, negative partisanship was more important on the Republican side because Republican elites, during and after the primaries, were far more divided than Democratic elites about their party's eventual nominee.

There was fierce resistance to Trump's candidacy from prominent Republicans prior to his nomination. Many Republican leaders, including the party's 2012 presidential nominee and both of its living former presidents, refused to endorse him even after the GOP convention.[23] Clinton, meanwhile, encountered no such opposition from Democratic elites and was the clear favorite of Democratic elected officials and party leaders around the country.[24] Given Trump's unpopularity with mainstream Republican elected officials and party leaders, one might have expected it to be very difficult to unite Republican voters behind his candidacy in the general election. However, almost all Republican voters were united by one thing: intense dislike of Democrats in general and Hillary Clinton in particular.

Campaigning and Governing in the Age of Trump

The changing voting patterns in 2016 represented, in important ways, a continuation of the electoral realignment that has been going on since the 1970s. The most dramatic shift in voting patterns in 2016 involved the growing alignment of partisanship with education among white voters. White voters with college degrees shifted toward the Democratic Party, while white voters without college degrees shifted toward the Republican Party. Donald Trump's candidacy clearly had something to do with this. His campaign slogan, "Make America Great Again," was directed at white working-class voters nostalgic for a time when people like themselves enjoyed greater influence and respect.

In his campaign rhetoric and even in his inaugural address, Trump constantly painted a portrait of a nation in steep decline—decline which only he could reverse. He repeatedly claimed, without evidence, that the unemployment rate in the United States was far higher than government statistics indicated, that violent crime in the nation's inner cities was soaring, and that the quality of health care available to most Americans had deteriorated badly since the adoption of the Affordable Care Act. He portrayed Islamic terrorism as a dire threat to ordinary Americans, even though very few Americans had actually been killed or injured in terrorist attacks by Islamic militants since 9/11.[25]

According to a survey conducted by the Pew Research Center in August 2016, a large majority of Trump's supporters shared his dark vision of the condition and direction of the nation. Fully 81 percent of Trump supporters, compared with only 19 percent of Clinton supporters, believed that "life for people like them" has gotten worse in the past fifty years. Moreover, 68 percent of Trump supporters, versus 30 percent of Clinton supporters, expected life for the next generation of Americans to be even worse.[26]

This deep pessimism appears to be based largely on unhappiness with the nation's changing demographics and values. Trump's appeals to racial resentment and xenophobia resonated with a large proportion of less-educated white voters, who were uncomfortable with the increasing diversity of American society. Likewise, his promise to appoint conservative judges who would limit the rights of gays and lesbians and curtail access to abortion appealed to religious conservatives upset with the American public's growing cultural liberalism. The same message that turned on large numbers of white working-class voters, however, turned off overwhelming majorities of African-American, Latino, Asian-American, and LGBT voters along with many white college graduates, especially women, who benefited from and welcomed these changes.

Perhaps more than any presidential candidate since George Wallace in 1968, and certainly more than any major party candidate in the past sixty years, Donald Trump reinforced some of the deepest social and cultural divisions within the American electorate. Yet those racial and religious cleavages existed, and voting patterns had begun to shift, long before 2016. The movement of white working-class voters from the Democratic camp to the Republican camp has been going on since at least 1964, when Lyndon Johnson firmly aligned the Democratic Party with the cause of civil rights for African-Americans. The movement of white evangelicals and other religious conservatives has been going on since at least 1980, when Ronald Reagan and the Republican Party came out for the repeal of *Roe v. Wade.*

Donald Trump's candidacy, and the entire 2016 presidential campaign, reinforced another long-standing trend in American electoral politics: the rise of negative partisanship. Voting based on hostility toward the opposing party may have reached an all-time high in 2016, but that doesn't mean we can expect it to diminish anytime soon. Early indications are that Trump's presidency is likely to extend and deepen this trend. Trump's actions during the transition, normally a time when newly elected presidents seek to reach across the party divide to former adversaries, were extraordinarily divisive. They included personal attacks on Democratic Party leaders, frequent questioning of the honesty and credibility of major media outlets, and unsubstantiated claims that massive voter fraud cost him a popular vote victory.[27]

His appointees to key White House and cabinet positions were, with few exceptions, hardline conservatives with little appeal to Democrats.[28] His cabinet had the largest proportion of white males since Ronald Reagan's presidency, along with the largest proportion of corporate CEOs and billionaires of any cabinet in history.[29] His appointment of his former campaign manager Steve Bannon, an individual with close ties to the racist and xenophobic "alt-right" movement, to a key White House advisory position alarmed Democrats, their progressive allies, and even some mainstream conservatives.[30] Unlike every other recent president, Trump nominated no members of the opposing party to his cabinet.

This pattern of divisive behavior continued during the first weeks of Trump's presidency, with continued attacks on the mainstream media and political opponents and the issuance of highly controversial executive orders on immigration, health care, and banking regulation. His inauguration was met with massive protest marches in cities across the nation and the world, with more than half a million demonstrating in Washington, D.C., and hundreds of thousands protesting in dozens of cities across the nation.[31] His executive order halting immigration from seven predominantly Muslim countries, including refugees arriving from Syria, led to hundreds of spontaneous demonstrations at airports across the United States as well as legal challenges. Trump fired the acting attorney general Sally Yates, a holdover from the Obama administration, after she ordered Justice Department officials not to enforce the order on the grounds that it was probably unconstitutional.[32]

Public opinion polls showed that reactions to Trump's performance were extraordinarily negative, and unprecedented for a newly elected president. The Gallup Poll found that his initial approval rating, 45 percent, was far lower than that of any newly elected president in the past sixty years, and his disapproval rating of 45 percent was far higher.[33] Other polls showed Trump's initial approval rating "upside down," with disapproval higher than approval. But these polls also found that opinions were sharply divided along party lines. A CNN Poll conducted just two weeks into his presidency found that 90 percent of Republicans approved of Trump's performance, while 89 percent of Democrats disapproved. Moreover, 76 percent of Republicans strongly approved of Trump's performance and 79 percent of Democrats strongly disapproved. Opinions were similarly divided among independents leaning toward a party: 88 percent of independent Republicans approved of Trump's performance while 89 percent of independent Democrats disapproved.[34]

Despite his overall unpopularity, Trump's solid support from Republican voters meant that Republicans in Congress, most of whom represent safe Republican constituencies, were under pressure to stick with the president. Democrats, on the other hand, faced mounting pressure from an increasingly frightened and angry base to oppose his actions whenever and wherever possible. Some commentators compared the wave of anti-Trump activism to a liberal version of the Tea Party movement that blossomed during the first year of the Obama administration.[35]

Based on these early trends, it appears very likely that ideological conflict and partisan hostility will reach new heights during the Trump years. Polarization and negative partisanship will remain major obstacles to any politician seeking support across party lines. Candidates must win their party's nomination by running a gauntlet of primaries and caucuses dominated by voters who are even more ideologically extreme and more hostile to the opposing party than their party's general election voters. As a result, any candidate conservative enough to win a Republican nomination will almost certainly be far too conservative to appeal to more than a handful of Democratic voters, and any candidate liberal enough to win a Democratic nomination will be far too liberal to appeal to more than a few Republican voters. Campaigns for major offices will probably continue to focus more on energizing and mobilizing their party's core supporters than on appealing to voters across the partisan divide.

Ideological polarization and negative partisanship will also obstruct efforts to work across party lines in government. Any such efforts will likely be greeted with deep suspicion by voters on both sides, especially the more attentive and politically active ones. Republicans in Congress will be under intense pressure to use their majorities in the House and Senate to ram through key items without input from Democrats. Democrats will be under intense pressure to use all of the tools at their disposal, including the filibuster in the Senate for as long as it remains in place, to oppose the GOP/Trump agenda. But given their very limited ability to resist congressional Republicans and Trump, Democrats and their liberal allies will likely turn increasingly to state governments under Democratic control and to the federal courts for assistance, as seen in the responses to President Trump's early executive orders. The Trump years are likely to witness the most intense partisan hostility in modern American history.

Notes

ONE
A New Age of Partisanship

1. Josh Kraushaar, "The Most Divided Congress Ever, at Least Until Next Year," *National Journal*, 2014 (http://www.nationaljournal.com/2013-vote -ratings/the-most-divided-congress-ever-at-least-until-next-year-2014 0206; accessed on March 27, 2015). See also Sean M. Theriault, *Party Polar- ization in Congress* (New York: Cambridge University Press, 2008); and Thomas E. Mann and Norman J. Ornstein, *It's Even Worse than It Looks: How the American Constitutional System Collided with the New Politics of Extremism* (New York: Basic Books, 2013).

2. Elahe Izadi, "Congress Sets Record for Voting Along Party Lines," *National Journal*, 2014 (http://www.nationaljournal.com/congress/congress-sets-rec ord-for-voting-along-party-lines-20140203; accessed on March 27, 2015).

3. Brandon L. Bartels, "The Sources and Consequences of Polarization in the U.S. Supreme Court," in *American Gridlock*, ed. James Thurber and Antoine Yoshinaka (New York: Cambridge University Press, in press). See also Tom S. Clark, "Measuring Ideological Polarization on the United States Supreme Court," *Political Research Quarterly* 62 (1), 2009: 146–157.

4. Boris Shor and Nolan McCarty, "The Ideological Mapping of American Legislatures," *American Political Science Review* 105 (3), 2011: 530–551.

5. Larry M. Bartels, "Partisanship and Voting Behavior, 1952–1996," *American

Journal of Political Science 44 (1), 2000: 35–50. See also Marc J. Hetherington, "Resurgent Mass Partisanship: The Role of Elite Polarization," *American Political Science Review* 95 (3), 2001: 619–631; and Donald Green, Bradley Palmquist, and Eric Schickler, *Partisan Hearts and Minds: Political Parties and the Social Identities of Voters* (New Haven: Yale University Press, 2002).

6. Jeffrey M. Jones, "In U.S., New Record 43% Are Political Independents," *Gallup Poll,* January 7, 2015 (http://www.gallup.com/poll/180440/new-rec ord-political-independents.aspx; accessed on June 13, 2015).

7. See Alan I. Abramowitz and Steven Webster, "The Rise of Negative Partisanship and the Nationalization of U.S. Elections in the 21st Century," *Electoral Studies* 41 (2006): 12–22.

8. Alan Abramowitz, "Partisan Nation: The Rise of Affective Partisanship in the American Electorate," in *The State of the Parties: The Changing Role of Contemporary American Parties,* 7th edition, ed. John C. Green, Daniel J. Coffey, and David B. Cohen (New York: Rowman and Littlefield, 2015), pp. 21–36. See also Shanto Iyengar, Gaurov Sood, and Yphtach Lelkes, "Affect, Not Ideology: A Social Identity Perspective on Polarization," *Public Opinion Quarterly* 76 (3), 2015: 405–431; and Gary C. Jacobson, *A Divider, Not a Uniter: George W. Bush and the American People* (New York: Pearson Longman, 2007).

9. Diana Mutz, "How the Mass Media Divide Us," in *Red and Blue Nation?* volume 1, ed. David Brady and Pietro Nivola (Stanford, Calif.: Hoover Institution Press, 2006), pp. 223–248. See also Markus Prior, *Post-Broadcast Democracy: How Media Choice Increases Inequality in Political Involvement and Polarizes Elections* (New York: Cambridge University Press, 2007); and Matthew S. Levendusky, "Why Do Partisan Media Polarize Voters?" *American Journal of Political Science* 57 (3), 2013: 611–623.

10. Positive partisans rate their own party farther above 50 degrees than they rate the opposing party below 50 degrees on the feeling thermometer; negative partisans rate the opposing party farther below 50 degrees than they rate their own party above 50 degrees.

11. Pew Research Center, "In Presidential Contest, Voters Say 'Basic Facts,' Not Just Policies Are in Dispute," *Pew Research Center,* October 14, 2016 (http:// assets.pewresearch.org/wp-content/uploads/sites/5/2016/10/14134143/10 -14-16-election-update-release.pdf).

12. Eduardo Bonilla-Silva, *Racism Without Racists: Color-Blind Racism and the Persistence of Racial Inequality in the United States* (Lanham, Md.: Rowman & Littlefield, 2006).

13. Michael Tesler and David O. Sears, *Obama's Race: The 2008 Election and the Dream of a Post-Racial America* (Chicago: University of Chicago Press, 2010). See also Donald R. Kinder and Allison Dale-Riddle, *The End of Race? Obama, 2008, and Racial Politics in America* (New Haven: Yale University Press, 2012),

and Michael Tesler, *Post-Racial or Most-Racial: Race and Politics in the Obama Era* (Chicago: University of Chicago Press, 2016).

14. William Frey, "Race, Immigration, and America's Changing Electorate," in *Red, Blue, and Purple America: The Future of Election Demographics*, ed. Ruy Teixeira (Washington, D.C.: Brookings Institution Press, 2008).

15. Hispanics made up a record 10 percent of the 2012 electorate according to the national exit poll.

16. Alan I. Abramowitz, *The Polarized Public? Why American Government Is So Dysfunctional* (New York: Pearson Longman, 2013), chapter 3.

17. See Chapter 7 for evidence that the ideological divide between Democratic and Republican voters remained very wide in 2016 despite the unusual nature of Donald Trump's candidacy.

18. Abramowitz, *The Polarized Public*, chapter 4. See also John Kenneth White, *The Values Divide: American Politics and Culture in Transition* (Washington, D.C.: CQ Press, 2002); and D. Sunshine Hillygus and Todd G. Shields, *The Persuadable Voter: Wedge Issues in Presidential Campaigns* (Princeton: Princeton University Press, 2008), chapter 5.

19. See, for example, John Cassidy, "Donald Trump's Dark, Dark Convention Speech," *The New Yorker*, July 22, 2016 (http://www.newyorker.com/news /john-cassidy/donald-trumps-dark-dark-convention-speech). For an analysis of Trump's inaugural address, see Ed Kilgore, "Trump's Dark, Weird Inaugural Campaign Speech," *New York Magazine*, January 20, 2017 (http://nymag .com/daily/intelligencer/2017/01/trumps-dark-weird-inaugural-campaign -speech.html).

20. Pew Research Center, "Clinton, Trump Supporters Have Starkly Different Views of a Changing Nation," *Pew Research Center*, August 18, 2016 (http:// www.people-press.org/2016/08/18/clinton-trump-supporters-have-starkly -different-views-of-a-changing-nation/).

21. Pew Research Center, "Political Polarization in the American Public," *Pew Research Center*, June 12, 2014 (http://www.people-press.org/files/2014/06 /6-12-2014-Political-Polarization-Release.pdf; accessed on June 13, 2015).

22. See Edgar E. Robinson, *They Voted for Roosevelt: The Presidential Vote, 1932–1944* (Stanford: Stanford University Press, 1947). See also Jean Edward Smith, *FDR* (New York: Random House, 2007).

TWO
The Decline of the New Deal Coalition

1. See David M. Kennedy, *Freedom from Fear: The American People in Depression and War* (New York: Oxford University Press, 1999).

2. For a description of Roosevelt's electoral coalition, see Edgar E. Robinson,

They Voted for Roosevelt: The Presidential Vote, 1932–1944 (Stanford, Calif.: Stanford University Press, 1947).

3. This theory was advanced most prominently by Horace Busby, a former White House advisor to Lyndon Johnson. Busby's theory was explained in an essay on the outlook for the 1988 presidential election by the well-known political commentator William Schneider. See Schneider, "An Insider's View of the Election," *The Atlantic Monthly*, 1988 (http://www.theatlantic.com/past /politics/policamp/insider.htm).

4. Kevin P. Phillips, *The Emerging Republican Majority* (New York: Arlington House, 1969).

5. See Bernard Cosman, *Five States for Goldwater: Continuity and Change in Southern Voting Patterns* (Tuscaloosa: University of Alabama Press, 1966).

6. See Earl Black and Merle Black, *The Rise of Southern Republicans* (Cambridge: Harvard University Press, 2002).

7. For an in-depth analysis of the role of African-Americans in southern politics during this era, see Donald R. Matthews, *Negroes and the New Southern Politics* (New York: Harcourt, 1966).

8. For a discussion of the struggle for black voting rights from the Reconstruction era through the 1960s, see Alexander Keyssar, *The Right to Vote: The Contested History of Democracy in the United States* (New York: Basic Books, 2000).

9. For a discussion of the rise of the religious right in the United States in response to changes in American society and culture, see William Martin, *With God on Our Side: The Rise of the Religious Right in America* (New York: Broadway Books, 1996).

10. See Gary Donaldson, *Liberalism's Last Hurrah: The Presidential Campaign of 1964* (New York: M.E. Sharpe, 2003).

11. For an insightful analysis of the role of George Wallace in American politics during this era, see Dan T. Carter, *The Politics of Rage: George Wallace, the Origins of the New Conservatism, and the Transformation of American Politics* (New York: Simon and Schuster, 1995).

12. Information on incumbency status for House districts is not available in ANES data for elections before 1972.

THREE

From Dealignment to Alignment

1. Helmut Norpoth and Jerrold G. Rusk, "Partisan Dealignment in the American Electorate: Itemizing the Deductions Since 1964," *American Political Science Review* 76 (3), 1982: 522–537; Edward G. Carmines, John P. McIver, and James A. Stimson, "Unrealized Partisanship: A Theory of Dealignment," *Journal of Politics* 49 (2), 1987: 376–400.

2. Richard Born, "Congressional Incumbency and the Rise of Split-Ticket Voting," *Legislative Studies Quarterly* 25 (3), 2000: 365–387.

3. See David R. Mayhew, *Divided We Govern: Party Control, Lawmaking, and Investigations, 1946–2002* (New Haven: Yale University Press, 2002).

4. See Gerald M. Pomper, F. Christopher Arterton, and Ross K. Baker, *The Election of 1992: Reports and Interpretations* (New York: Chatham House, 1992).

5. James E. Campbell, "The Presidential Pulse and the 1994 Midterm Congressional Election," *Journal of Politics* 59 (3), 1997: 830–857. See also Alan I. Abramowitz, "The End of the Democratic Era? 1994 and the Future of Congressional Election Research," *Political Research Quarterly* 48 (4), 1995: 873–890, and David W. Brady, John F. Cogan, Brian J. Gaines, and Douglas Rivers, "The Perils of Presidential Support: How the Republicans Took the House in the 1994 Midterm Elections," *Political Behavior* 18 (4), 1996: 345–367.

6. See Thomas Byrne Edsall with Mary D. Edsall, *Chain Reaction: The Impact of Race, Rights, and Taxes on American Politics.* New York: W.W. Norton and Company, 1992.

7. William H. Frey, *Diversity Explosion: How Changing Racial Demographics Are Remaking America* (Washington, D.C.: Brookings Institution Press, 2015).

8. See Pew Research Center, "America's Changing Religious Landscape: Christians Decline Sharply as Share of Population; Unaffiliated and Other Faiths Continue to Grow," *Pew Research Center,* May 12, 2015 (http://www.pewforum.org/files/2015/05/RLS-08-26-full-report.pdf).

9. See Geoffrey Layman, *The Great Divide: Religious and Cultural Conflict in American Politics* (New York: Columbia University Press, 2001); see also John Kenneth White, *The Values Divide: American Politics and Culture in Transition* (Washington, D.C.: CQ Press, 2003).

10. By controlling for short-term factors favoring one party or the other in a specific presidential election, this measure provides a more accurate gauge of the underlying partisan orientation of House districts than simply using the winner of the presidential election.

FOUR

The Changing Political Geography of the United States

1. Data for 1974–1982 come from CBS/New York Times polls that were compiled by political scientists Gerald Wright, Robert Erikson, and John McIver. By merging nine years of surveys, they obtained enough data to produce reliable estimates of party strength in forty-eight states and the District of Columbia—Alaska and Hawaii were not included in the CBS/New York Times surveys during this period. Data for 2012 come from responses compiled by the Gallup polling organization in connection with their daily track-

ing poll. In this case, combining data on respondents interviewed over the course of an entire year makes it possible to produce reliable estimates of party strength in all fifty states and the District of Columbia. For a description of the data set, see Gerald C. Wright, Robert S. Erikson, and John P. McIver, "Measuring State Partisanship and Ideology with Survey Data," *Journal of Politics* 47 (2), June 1985: 469–489. For Gallup's 2012 state party identification data, see Lydia Saad, "In the U.S., Blue States Outnumber Red States, 20 to 12," *Gallup Poll*, January 30, 2013 (http://www.gallup.com/poll /160175/blue-states-outnumber-red-states.aspx). For Gallup's 2012 state ideology data, see Frank Newport, "Alabama, North Dakota, Wyoming Most Conservative States," *Gallup Poll*, February 1, 2013 (http://www.gallup.com /poll/160196/alabama-north-dakota-wyoming-conservative-states.aspx).

2. This view of the nature of party identification was originally set forth by Angus Campbell, Philip E. Converse, Warren E. Miller, and Donald E. Stokes in *The American Voter* (New York: John Wiley & Sons, 1960, chapters 6–7). A more recent statement of this position can be found in Donald P. Green, Bradley Palmquist, and Eric Schickler, *Partisan Hearts and Minds: Political Parties and the Social Identities of Voters* (New Haven: Yale University Press, 2002). For a contrasting view of the stability of partisanship and its relationship with ideology in recent elections, see Alan I. Abramowitz and Kyle L. Saunders, "Ideological Realignment in the U.S. Electorate," *Journal of Politics* 60 (3), August 1998: 634–652. See also Joseph Bafumi and Robert Y. Shapiro, "A New Partisan Voter," *Journal of Politics* 71 (1), January 2009: 1–24.

FIVE
The New American Electorate

1. On racial division, M. V. Hood III, Quentin Kidd, and Irwin L. Morris, "The Reintroduction of the *Elephas Maximus* to the Southern United States: The Rise of Republican State Parties, 1960 to 2000," *American Politics Research* 32 (1), 2004: 68–101. On ideological division, Alan I. Abramowitz and Kyle L. Saunders, "Exploring the Bases of Partisanship in the American Electorate: Social Identity vs. Ideology," *Political Research Quarterly* 59 (2), 2006: 175–187. See also Gary C. Jacobson, *A Divider, Not a Uniter: George W. Bush and the American People* (New York: Pearson Longman, 2007); Alan I. Abramowitz, *The Polarized Public: Why Our Government Is So Dysfunctional* (New York: Pearson Longman, 2013); Gary C. Jacobson, "How the Economy and Partisanship Shaped the 2012 Presidential and Congressional Elections," *Political Science Quarterly* 128 (1), 2013: 1–38. On cultural division, John K. White, *The Values Divide* (New York: Chatham House, 2003). See also Mark D. Brewer and Jeffrey M. Stonecash, *Split: Class and Cultural Divides in American*

Politics (Washington, D.C.: Congressional Quarterly Press, 2007); Sunshine D. Hillygus and Todd G. Shields, *The Persuadable Voter: Wedge Issues in Presidential Campaigns* (Princeton: Princeton University Press, 2008), chapter 5.

2.   Alan I. Abramowitz, Brad Alexander, and Matthew Gunning, "Incumbency, Redistricting, and the Decline of Competition in U.S. House Elections," *The Journal of Politics* 68 (1), 2006: 75–88.

3.   Seth E. Masket, Jonathan Winburn, and Gerald C. Wright, "The Gerrymanders Are Coming! Legislative Redistricting Won't Affect Competition or Polarization Much, No Matter Who Does It," *PS: Political Science and Politics* 45 (1), 2012: 39–43.

4.   Bill Bishop, *The Big Sort: Why the Clustering of Like-Minded Americans Is Tearing Us Apart* (New York: Houghton-Mifflin, 2008).

5.   Gary C. Jacobson, "How the Economy and Partisanship Shaped the 2012 Presidential and Congressional Elections," *Political Science Quarterly* 128 (1), 2013: 1–38.

6.   Stephen Ansolabehere, Jonathan Rodden, and James M. Snyder, "Purple America," *The Journal of Economic Perspectives* 20 (2), 2006: 97–118. See also Morris P. Fiorina, Samuel J. Abrams, and Jeremy C. Pope, *Culture War? The Myth of a Polarized America*, 3rd edition (New York: Pearson Longman, 2011); Matthew S. Levendusky and Jeremy C. Pope, "Red States vs. Blue States: Going Beyond the Mean," *Public Opinion Quarterly* 75 (2), 2011: 227–248; Morris P. Fiorina and Samuel J. Abrams, *Disconnect: The Breakdown of Representation in American Politics* (Norman: University of Oklahoma Press, 2009).

7.   Pamela J. Conover and Stanley Feldman, "The Origins and Meaning of Liberal/Conservative Self-Identifications," *American Journal of Political Science* 25 (4), 1981: 617–645.

8.   Philip E. Converse, "The Nature of Belief Systems in Mass Publics," in *Ideology and Discontent*, ed. David E. Apter (New York: The Free Press, 1964).

9.   Shanto Iyengar, Gaurav Sood, and Yphtach Lelkes, "Affect, Not Ideology: A Social Identity Perspective on Polarization," *Public Opinion Quarterly* 76 (3), 2012: 405–431. See also Lilliana Mason, "'I Disrespectfully Disagree': The Differential Effects of Partisan Sorting on Social and Issue Polarization," *American Journal of Political Science* 58 (3), 2012: 1–18.

10.   Morris P. Fiorina, Samuel J. Abrams, and Jeremy C. Pope, *Culture War? The Myth of a Polarized America*, 3rd edition (New York: Pearson Longman, 2011), pp. 25–32.

11.   Morris P. Fiorina and Samuel J. Abrams, *Disconnect: The Breakdown of Representation in American Politics* (Norman: University of Oklahoma Press, 2009).

12.   David R. Mayhew, *Divided We Govern: Party Control, Lawmaking, and Investigations, 1946–1990* (New Haven: Yale University Press, 1991).

13.   Thomas E. Mann and Norman J. Ornstein, "Let's Just Say It: The Republicans Are the Problem," *Washington Post*, April 27, 2012 (http://www.washing

tonpost.com/opinions/lets-just-say-it-the-republicans-are-the-problem
/2012/04/27/gIQAxCVUlT_story.html).

14. Alan I. Abramowitz, *The Disappearing Center: Engaged Citizens, Polarization and American Democracy* (New Haven: Yale University Press, 2010).

15. Markus Prior, *Post-Broadcast Democracy: How Media Choice Increases Inequality in Political Involvement and Polarizes Elections* (Cambridge: Cambridge University Press, 2007).

SIX

White Racial Resentment and the Rise of Donald Trump

1. See Leon Neyfakh, "How Nate Silver Missed Donald Trump," *Slate*, January 25, 2016 (http://www.slate.com/articles/news_and_politics/politics/2016/01 /nate_silver_said_donald_trump_had_no_shot_where_did_he_go_wrong .html). For Silver's own explanation of how he went wrong, see Nate Silver, "How I Acted Like a Pundit and Screwed Up on Donald Trump," *FiveThirty- Eight*, May 18, 2016 (http://fivethirtyeight.com/features/how-i-acted-like-a -pundit-and-screwed-up-on-donald-trump/). See also Nate Cohn, "What I Got Wrong About Donald Trump," *New York Times*, May 4, 2016 (http:// www.nytimes.com/2016/05/05/upshot/what-i-got-wrong-about-donald -trump.html?ref=topics&_r=0).

2. Marty Cohen, David Karol, Hans Noel, and John Zaller, *The Party Decides: Presidential Nominations Before and After Reform* (Chicago: University of Chi- cago, Press, 2008). For critical perspectives on this theory, see Norm Orn- stein, "Maybe This Time Really Is Different," *The Atlantic*, August 21, 2015 (http://www.theatlantic.com/politics/archive/2015/08/maybe-this-time -really-is-different/401900/). See also Andrew Prokop, "Political Scientists Think 'The Party' Will Stop Trump. They Shouldn't Be So Sure," *Vox*, Sep- tember 23, 2015 (http://www.vox.com/2015/9/23/9352273/party-decides -trump-sanders). For my own perspective on this issue, see Ezra Klein, "Why One Political Scientist Thinks Donald Trump Might Actually Win," *Vox*, November 25, 2015 (http://www.vox.com/2015/11/25/9800174/why-one -political-scientist-thinks-donald-trump-might-actually-win).

3. See David A. Graham, "Which Republicans Oppose Donald Trump: A Cheat Sheet," *The Atlantic*, November 6, 2016 (http://www.theatlantic.com /politics/archive/2016/11/where-republicans-stand-on-donald-trump-a -cheat-sheet/481449/). See also Aaron Bycoffe, "The Endorsement Primary," *FiveThirtyEight*, June 7, 2016 (https://projects.fivethirtyeight.com/2016-en dorsement-primary/).

4. See Jack Rasmus, "Trump, Trade, and Working Class Discontent," *Counter- punch*, July 22, 2016 (http://www.counterpunch.org/2016/07/22/trump-trade

-and-working-class-discontent/). See also Jon Hilsenrath and Bob Davis, "The Great Unraveling: Election 2016 Is Propelled by American Economy's Failed Promises," *Wall Street Journal*, July 7, 2016 (http://www.wsj.com/articles /election-2016-is-propelled-by-the-american-economys-failed-promises -1467909580); and Torstein Bell, "The Invisible Economic Catastrophe that Donald Trump Spotted," *New Statesman*, November 10, 2016 (http://www .newstatesman.com/politics/staggers/2016/11/invisible-economic-catastro phe-donald-trump-spotted).

5. Peter W. Stevenson, "Donald Trump Loves the 'Poorly Educated'—And Just About Everyone Else in Nevada," *Washington Post*, February 24, 2016 (https:// www.washingtonpost.com/news/the-fix/wp/2016/02/24/donald-trump -loves-the-poorly-educated-and-just-about-everyone-else-in-nevada/?utm _term=.b49741f8342d).

6. Christopher Ingraham, "Two New Studies Find Racial Anxiety Is the Biggest Driver of Support for Trump," *Washington Post*, June 6, 2016 (https://www. washingtonpost.com/news/wonk/wp/2016/06/06/racial-anxiety-is-a-huge -driver-of-support-for-donald-trump-two-new-studies-find/?utm_term =.484b5ac8ea3d). See also Matthew Yglesias, "Why I Don't Think It Makes Sense to Attribute Trump's Support to Economic Anxiety," *Vox*, August 15, 2016 (http://www.vox.com/2016/8/15/12462760/trump-resentment-economic -anxiety).

7. Ronald B. Rapoport, Alan I. Abramowitz, and Walter J. Stone, "Why Trump Was Inevitable," *New York Review of Books*, June 23, 2016, pp. 9–10; see also Molly Ball, "Donald Trump and the Politics of Fear," *The Atlantic*, September 2, 2016 (http://www.theatlantic.com/politics/archive/2016/09/donald -trump-and-the-politics-of-fear/498116/).

8. Eric Bradner, "Donald Trump Stumbles on David Duke, KKK," *CNN*, February 29, 2016 (http://www.cnn.com/2016/02/28/politics/donald-trump-white -supremacists/).

9. Michael Barbaro, "Donald Trump Clung to 'Birther' Lie for Years, and Still Isn't Apologetic," *New York Times*, September 16, 2016 (http://www.nytimes .com/2016/09/17/us/politics/donald-trump-obama-birther.html).

10. See Josh Clinton and Carrie Roush, "Poll: Persistent Partisan Divide over 'Birther' Question," *NBC News*, August 10, 2016 (http://www.nbcnews.com /politics/2016-election/poll-persistent-partisan-divide-over-birther-question -n627446).

11. Andrew Kaczynski, "Trump Questioned Obama Birth Certificate in 2014, Despite Campaign Statement," *BuzzFeedNews*, September 16, 2016 (https:// www.buzzfeed.com/andrewkaczynski/trump-questioned-obama-birth-cer tificate-in-2014-despite-cam?utm_term=.ld4ZPLJXN#.liOad97DQ).

12. See Jonathan Martin, Jim Rutenberg, and Maggie Haberman, "Trump Appoints Media Firebrand to Run Campaign," *New York Times*, August 17, 2016

(http://www.nytimes.com/2016/08/18/us/politics/donald-trump-stephen
-bannon-paul-manafort.html). See also Michael D. Shear, Maggie Haberman,
and Michael S. Schmidt, "Critics See Stephen Bannon, Trump's Pick for
Strategist, as Voice of Racism," *New York Times*, November 14, 2016 (http://
www.nytimes.com/2016/11/15/us/politics/donald-trump-presidency.html).

13. Pew Research Center, "Clinton, Trump Supporters Have Starkly Different
Views of a Changing Nation," *Pew Research Center*, August 18, 2016 (http://
www.people-press.org/2016/08/18/1-voters-general-election-preferences/).

14. See Edward G. Carmines, Paul M. Sniderman, and Beth C. Easter, "On the
Meaning, Measurement, and Implications of Racial Resentment," *Annals of
the American Academy of Political and Social Science* 634 (March 2011): 98–116.

15. See Michael Tesler and David O. Sears, *Obama's Race: The 2008 Election and
the Dream of a Post-Racial America* (Chicago: University of Chicago Press,
2010).

SEVEN

Negative Partisanship and the Triumph of Trump

1. Polls conducted prior to the election provided mixed evidence concerning
the impact of the Comey letter. See, however, Sean McElwee, Matt McDer-
mott, and Will Jordan, "Four Pieces of Evidence Showing FBI Director
James Comey Cost Clinton the Election," *Vox*, January 11, 2017 (http://
www.vox.com/the-big-idea/2017/1/11/14215930/comey-email-election
-clinton-campaign). See also Rebecca Savransky, "Nate Silver: Clinton Almost Certainly Would've Won Before FBI Letter," *The Hill*, December 11,
2016 (http://thehill.com/homenews/campaign/309871-nate-silver-clinton
-almost-certainly-wouldve-won-if-election-were-before). On the impact of
the WikiLeaks releases of hacked DNC emails, see Harry Enten, "How
Much Did WikiLeaks Hurt Hillary Clinton?" *FiveThirtyEight*, December
23, 2016 (https://fivethirtyeight.com/features/wikileaks-hillary-clinton/).

2. See also Christopher Ingraham, "Two New Studies Find Racial Anxiety Is
the Biggest Driver of Support for Trump," *Washington Post Wonkblog*, June 6,
2016 (https://www.washingtonpost.com/news/wonk/wp/2016/06/06/racial
-anxiety-is-a-huge-driver-of-support-for-donald-trump-two-new-studies
-find/?utm_term=.0c6ed499b28c).

3. Nate Silver, "The Mythology of Trump's Working Class Support," *FiveThirty-
Eight*, May 3, 2016 (https://fivethirtyeight.com/features/the-mythology-of
-trumps-working-class-support/).

4. See David Lauter, "Trump Is Now the Least Popular American Politician
in Three Decades," *Los Angeles Times*, April 1, 2016 (http://www.latimes.com
/politics/la-na-trump-unpopularity-20160401-story.html).

5. Alan I. Abramowitz, *The Polarized Public: Why American Government Is So Dysfunctional* (New York: Pearson Longman, 2013), chapter 5.

6. For an analysis of the regional realignment of the parties since the 1960s and its consequences, see Earl Black and Merle Black, *Divided America: The Ferocious Power Struggle in American Politics* (New York: Simon and Schuster, 2007).

7. See Amy Walter, "How Trump Broke the Blue Wall," *Cook Political Report*, December 9, 2016 (http://cookpolitical.com/story/10191).

8. Nate Cohn, "Why Trump Had an Edge in the Electoral College," *New York Times Upshot Blog*, December 19, 2016 (https://www.nytimes.com/2016/12/19/upshot/why-trump-had-an-edge-in-the-electoral-college.html?_r=0).

9. See Jack Rasmus, "Trump, Trade, and Working Class Discontent," *Counterpunch*, July 22, 2016 (http://www.counterpunch.org/2016/07/22/trump-trade-and-working-class-discontent/). See also Jon Hilsenrath and Bob Davis, "The Great Unraveling: Election 2016 Is Propelled by American Economy's Failed Promises," *Wall Street Journal*, July 7, 2016 (https://www.wsj.com/articles/election-2016-is-propelled-by-the-american-economys-failed-promises-1467909580). See also Torstein Bell, "The Invisible Economic Catastrophe that Donald Trump Spotted," *New Statesman*, November 10, 2016 (http://www.newstatesman.com/politics/staggers/2016/11/invisible-economic-catastrophe-donald-trump-spotted).

10. See Christopher Ingraham, "Two New Studies Find Racial Anxiety Is the Biggest Driver of Support for Trump," *Washington Post*, June 6, 2016 (https://www.washingtonpost.com/news/wonk/wp/2016/06/06/racial-anxiety-is-a-huge-driver-of-support-for-donald-trump-two-new-studies-find/?utm_term=.101abdeofea0). See also Matthew Yglesias, "Why I Don't Think It Makes Sense to Attribute Trump Support to Economic Anxiety," *Vox*, August 15, 2016 (http://www.vox.com/2016/8/15/12462760/trump-resentment-economic-anxiety). For evidence that Trump's attacks on Mexican immigrants and Muslims were crucial to his support among Republican primary voters, see Ronald B. Rapoport, Alan I. Abramowitz, and Walter J. Stone, "Why Trump Was Inevitable," *New York Review of Books*, June 23, 2016, pp. 8–10; see also Molly Ball, "Donald Trump and the Politics of Fear," *The Atlantic*, September 2, 2016 (https://www.theatlantic.com/politics/archive/2016/09/donald-trump-and-the-politics-of-fear/498116/).

11. Michael Tesler, "Economic Anxiety Isn't Driving Racial Resentment. Racial Resentment Is Driving Economic Anxiety," *Washington Post Monkey Cage Blog*, August 22, 2016 (https://www.washingtonpost.com/news/monkey-cage/wp/2016/08/22/economic-anxiety-isnt-driving-racial-resentment-racial-resentment-is-driving-economic-anxiety/?utm_term=.b53cf677a392).

12. See Michael Tesler, "The Education Gap Among Whites This Year Wasn't About Education. It Was About Race," *Washington Post Monkey Cage Blog*, November 16, 2016 (https://www.washingtonpost.com/news/monkey-cage

/wp/2016/11/16/the-education-gap-among-whites-this-year-wasnt-about
-education-it-was-about-race/?utm_term=.5d537d018df5).

13. The measure of racial and ethnic resentment combines the traditional four-item racial-resentment scale with six items measuring support or opposition to immigration. I combined these into one scale because the correlation between the racial-resentment scale and the anti-immigration scale was a very strong .65. Moreover, a factor analysis of the ten items indicates that they are measuring a single underlying dimension and the ten-item racial/ethnic resentment scale has a Cronbach's alpha of .87. The misogyny scale is based on three items measuring negative or hostile attitudes toward women.

14. See Gary Legum, "Trump vs. the GOP: His Economic Push Is 180 Degrees from the Party's Long-Held Platform," *Salon*, September 16, 2016 (http://www.salon.com/2016/09/16/trump-vs-the-gop-his-economic-push-is-180-degrees-from-the-partys-long-held-platform/).

15. John Harwood, "On Trade, Donald Trump Breaks with G.O.P., and Economists," *New York Times*, July 5, 2016 (https://www.nytimes.com/2016/07/06/us/politics/donald-trump-trade.html?_r=0).

16. See Harry Enten, "What Bernie Sanders Meant," *FiveThirtyEight*, July 12, 2016 (http://fivethirtyeight.com/features/what-bernie-sanders-meant/).

17. Philip E. Converse, "The Nature of Belief Systems in Mass Publics," in *Ideology and Discontent*, ed. David E. Apter (London: The Free Press of Glencoe, 1964).

18. See Shanto Iyengar and Sean J. Westwood, "Fear and Loathing Across Party Lines: New Evidence on Group Polarization," *American Journal of Political Science* 59 (3), 2015: 690–707.

19. Alan I. Abramowitz and Steven Webster, "The Rise of Negative Partisanship and the Nationalization of U.S. Elections in the 21st Century," *Electoral Studies* 41 (2016): 12–22.

20. Lydia Saad, "Trump and Clinton Finish with Historically Poor Images," *Gallup Poll*, November 8, 2016 (http://www.gallup.com/poll/197231/trump-clinton-finish-historically-poor-images.aspx).

21. Frank Newport and Andrew Dugan, "One in Four Americans Dislike Both Presidential Candidates," *Gallup Poll*, July 12, 2016 (http://www.gallup.com/opinion/polling-matters/187652/one-four-americans-dislike-presidential-candidates.aspx).

22. Lydia Saad, "Aversion to Other Candidate Key Factor in 2016 Vote Choice," *Gallup Poll*, October 6, 2016 (http://www.gallup.com/poll/196172/aversion-candidate-key-factor-2016-vote-choice.aspx).

23. See Karen Younish, Larry Buchanan, and Alicia Parlapiano, "More than 160 Republican Leaders Don't Support Donald Trump. Here's When They Reached Their Breaking Point," *New York Times*, October 9, 2016 (https://

www.nytimes.com/interactive/2016/08/29/us/politics/at-least-110-republican
-leaders-wont-vote-for-donald-trump-heres-when-they-reached-their
-breaking-point.html).

24. Harry Enten, "Hillary Clinton Is the Most Establishment-Approved Candidate on Record," *FiveThirtyEight*, November 13, 2015 (https://fivethirtyeight
.com/features/hillary-clinton-is-the-most-establishment-approved-candidate
-on-record/).

25. See, for example, John Cassidy, "Donald Trump's Dark, Dark Convention Speech," *The New Yorker*, July 22, 2016 (http://www.newyorker.com/news
/john-cassidy/donald-trumps-dark-dark-convention-speech). For an analysis of Trump's inaugural address, see Ed Kilgore, "Trump's Dark, Weird Inaugural Campaign Speech," *New York Magazine*, January 20, 2017 (http://
nymag.com/daily/intelligencer/2017/01/trumps-dark-weird-inaugural
-campaign-speech.html).

26. Pew Research Center, "Clinton, Trump Supporters Have Starkly Different Views of a Changing Nation," *Pew Research Center*, August 18, 2016 (http://
www.people-press.org/2016/08/18/clinton-trump-supporters-have-starkly
-different-views-of-a-changing-nation/).

27. See Stephen Collinson, "Tumult Surrounds Trump Days Ahead of His Presidency," *CNN*, January 17, 2017 (http://www.cnn.com/2017/01/16/politics
/donald-trump-presidency/).

28. Matthew Cooper, "Donald Trump Is Building the Most Conservative Presidential Cabinet in U.S. History," *Newsweek*, December 9, 2016 (http://www
.newsweek.com/trump-cabinet-picks-nominees-conservative-530477).

29. Lisa Lerer and Julie Pace, "Trump's Cabinet Is Really White and Really Rich," *Salon*, December 16, 2016 (www.salon.com/2016/12/16/trump-lags
-predecessors-on-diversity-as-he-picks-cabinet).

30. Adam Kelsey and Veronica Stracqualursi, "Why Trump's Appointment of Steve Bannon Has Raised so Many Alarms," *ABC News*, November 15, 2016 (http://abcnews.go.com/Politics/trumps-appointment-steve-bannon
-raised-alarms/story?id=43554212).

31. Mallory Shelbourne, "Women's Marches Draw Huge Crowds as Trump Takes Office," *The Hill*, January 21, 2017 (http://thehill.com/homenews
/315488-womens-marches-take-hold-of-cities-across-world).

32. Alicia Caldwell and Catherine Lucey, "Trump Ousts Acting Attorney General as Outcry Grows," *ABC News*, January 30, 2017 (http://abcnews.go.com
/Politics/wireStory/white-house-defends-immigration-order-face-protests
-45138177).

33. Lydia Saad, "Trump Sets New Low Point for Inaugural Approval Rating," *Gallup Poll*, January 23, 2017 (http://www.gallup.com/poll/202811/trump-sets
-new-low-point-inaugural-approval-rating.aspx).

34. Jennifer Agiesta, "First Trump Approval Rating Lags Behind Past Presidents," *CNN*, February 3, 2017 (http://www.cnn.com/2017/02/03/politics/donald-trump-approval-rating/index.html).

35. See Ronald Brownstein, "Are Liberals Launching Their Own Tea Party?" *The Atlantic*, January 26, 2017 (https://www.theatlantic.com/politics/archive/2017/01/are-liberals-launching-their-own-tea-party/514403/).

Index

abortion, 14–15, 27, 109, 170; attitudinal consistency and, 113–114;
growing availability of, 53; partisan
divide on, 10, 11, 12, 57–58, 107,
117, 128; social welfare issues
linked to, 107–108; as state-level
issue, 17
activist government, 13, 112, 117, 163
adoption rights, 107
affective polarization, 109–112,
164–168
affirmative action, 125
Affordable Care Act (2010), 10, 13, 14,
163, 164, 169
African-Americans, 8–9, 14, 18, 82–83,
170; attitudes toward, 105, 129;
cultural issues deemphasized by,
53–54; in Deep South vs. Rim
South, 24–25, 126; Democratic
appeals to, 30; New Deal policies

aimed at, 19–20; northward
migration of, 21, 23; party identification among, 16, 22, 38; party
loyalty among, 33; as share of
electorate, 126, 148, 150; voting
restrictions on, 20, 23–24, 27
Alabama, 21, 76, 78, 124–125; black
disenfranchisement in, 25
"alt-right" movement, 124, 171
Arizona, 148
Arkansas, 24–25, 45, 74, 144
Asian-Americans, 8–9, 14, 126
attitudinal consistency, 112–113

Bannon, Stephen, 124, 171
birth control, 53, 163, 164
birtherism, 123–124, 140, 143, 153
blue-collar voters. See working-class
voters
Busby, Horace, 178n3